Occupational Identity

OCCUPATIONAL IDENTITY

Journeys of Minoritized Occupational
Therapists Across Race, Religion, and Culture

Alaa Abou-Arab and Erica V. Herrera

with the
Coalition of Occupational Therapy Advocates for Diversity

Jessica Kingsley Publishers
London and Philadelphia

First published in Great Britain in 2024 by Jessica Kingsley Publishers
An imprint of John Murray Press

1

A CIP catalogue record for this title is available from the
British Library and the Library of Congress

ISBN 978 1 83997 820 3
eISBN 978 1 83997 821 0

Printed and bound in the United States by Integrated Books International

Jessica Kingsley Publishers' policy is to use papers that are natural,
renewable and recyclable products and made from wood grown in
sustainable forests. The logging and manufacturing processes are expected
to conform to the environmental regulations of the country of origin.

Jessica Kingsley Publishers
Carmelite House
50 Victoria Embankment
London EC4Y 0DZ

www.jkp.com

John Murray Press
Part of Hodder & Stoughton Ltd
An Hachette Company

Contents

FOREWORD BY THE COALITION OF OCCUPATIONAL
THERAPY ADVOCATES FOR DIVERSITY 7

PROLOGUE: OUR BACKGROUNDS AND OUR JOURNEYS:
EDSON'S OCCUPATIONAL THERAPY JOURNEY, IN HIS WORDS. . 11

Introduction 15

1. There's No Part of Me That Desires to be the Outlier 21
   ERICA V. HERRERA 21

2. An Onus on Justice 31
   ALAA ABOU-ARAB 31

3. Amalgamate 39
   ERICA V. HERRERA 39

4. No, I Was Not Surprised 47
   ERICA V. HERRERA 47

5. I Choose to Love 57
   ALAA ABOU-ARAB 57

6. I Have Always Been an OT 63
   ALAA ABOU-ARAB 63

7. Kiddush Hashem 71
   ERICA V. HERRERA 71

8. More Than the Model Minority 81

ALAA ABOU-ARAB 81

9. Mental Resilience 91

ERICA V. HERRERA 91

10. Practice with Integrity 101

ERICA V. HERRERA 101

11. A Mestizo of Self-Discovery 111

ALAA ABOU-ARAB 111

12. I am Proud to be an OT 119

ALAA ABOU-ARAB 119

13. I Was Always the Only One 127

ALAA ABOU-ARAB 127

14. Hey, My Name is Alaa, I'm Your OT Today 135

ERICA V. HERRERA 135

Foreword

Alaa and Erica met in 2020 during a convening of the Occupational Therapy Association of California (OTAC). During this time, OTAC was also forming a DEI (diversity, equity, inclusion) committee, and the two served on the committee together. It was in this space of professional organizing that Erica and Alaa soon realized their unified passion for action in work focused on *justice*, *equity*, *diversity*, and *inclusion* (JEDI) within the profession of occupational therapy (OT). Together, they generated the idea of "putting stories in our hands," creating a platform for occupational therapy practitioners (OTPs) from historically minoritized backgrounds and others who identify with the profession where they could experience radical inclusion and belonging, new learning and unlearning, with intention and empathy. Their collective hope was for those who engaged with these narratives to glean critical insights of themselves and make deeper connections with others through their lived experiences and universal love of the authors who share these stories for learning.

The Coalition of Occupational Therapy Advocates for Diversity (COTAD) was established in 2014 as a grassroots organization to address the need for greater diversity within the OT profession. The organization has grown tremendously since its early days, as has its mission and vision. Now, as an internationally recognized non-profit organization, COTAD operates as a group of individuals from across the United States all working toward a common goal of promoting anti-racism, anti-oppression, and JEDI within the occupational therapy workforce, and increasing the ability of OT practitioners to serve diverse populations effectively. Over the past decade, COTAD has been amplified by students, practitioners, and educators as an organization committed to raising awareness of systemic injustices and inspiring collective action. COTAD has learned that when communities take the time to understand the intersecting identities of its members, they gain insight into their experiences, struggles, and achievements. *Occupational Identity* offers a powerful glimpse into personal narratives of resilience, identity, growth, and the pursuit of meaning. COTAD endorses this book because these stories empower readers to gain empathy, broaden their understanding of different perspectives, and reflect on their own lives to serve the greater good of humanity.

In the fall of 2021, COTAD reached out to Alaa to inquire about a potential collaboration as part of its effort to organize ideas to better support Middle Eastern OT community members. From discussions centered on the need for awareness of systemic injustices and the intersection of occupational identity and the work of OT practitioners came the idea of a partnership on the book Alaa and Erica were gearing up to write. Given the alignment of this plan with the mission of COTAD, it was determined that COTAD would contribute to and endorse this book, based on the shared vision and goals for collective action through storytelling as well as the desire of all involved to elevate the voices of those othered in the profession.

As you read this book, we encourage you to reflect on your own experiences and biases as they impact the way you view and interact in this world. We also encourage you to keep an open mind and consider how *you* can make our profession a space of inclusion and equity. When we take the time to understand the identities of individuals, we gain insight into their experiences, struggles, and achievements. This understanding fosters empathy, allowing us to relate to their experiences and challenges. Empathy is a powerful tool in combating racism, as it promotes compassion and a sense of shared humanity. Furthermore, when we actively seek to learn about and understand the experiences of people from different backgrounds, we create opportunities for dialogue, mutual respect, and collaboration. By understanding the diverse identities of others, we can break down stereotypes, recognizing that individuals within a "group" are not homogeneous but have unique experiences, perspectives, and qualities.

Thus, engaging with the stories in this book will be uniquely experienced by every reader. Some may feel a deep connection to various identities and dreams of future achievements yet realized, and others may feel tensions between their lived experiences and those of the authors as they reconcile their differences as well as commonalities. We express the utmost gratitude to those who shared their stories; your vulnerability is respected, appreciated, and cared for. Sharing your stories will have a tremendous impact on the readers.

Thank you to the authors who brought this vision to life and worked to make sure their vision came to fruition. We thank you for allowing COTAD to be a part of this journey. We value your work and the impact this book will have on bringing the profession closer to the American Occupational Therapy Association's Vision 2025.

May this book inspire you to practice cultural humility and engage with your colleagues and clients holistically. Lead with love, lead with action, create a sense of belonging in the spaces you occupy, and push forward for equity and inclusion for *all*.

In solidarity.

*The Coalition of Occupational Therapy
Advocates for Diversity (COTAD)*

Our Backgrounds and Our Journeys: Edson's Occupational Therapy Journey, in His Words

OT school

I was anxious, and I was nervous for a lot of reasons. I needed to be the best that I could be, and I needed to graduate so that I could start my career. Knowing the demographics about the place and the demographics about the profession, I had a predetermined expectation of the people whom I was going to be around and who would be a part of my class. I was expecting to be one of the few Mexican male students in my cohort. So, I was thinking, "Man, I'm not going to make a lot of guy friends." It was anatomy, the first day. I'm sitting there in the middle section of the lecture hall and they're passing out the anatomy notebooks to all the students. So, I get up and I walk down the steps. I'm just in line and then I see a guy, and he's wearing this Chivas backpack! I was just mind-blown because I was not expecting that. Soccer is like religion in Mexico. The most popular teams are America and Chivas; consequently, they are the main rivals. Chivas fans are like working-class people, very traditional. Only Mexican players can play in this team. The team that I follow has different values. Club America represents the powerful and are considered the rich team in the Mexican soccer league. They are people who will try and do whatever they need to in order to win. So, the two teams don't click. I was not expecting many Mexican students in my cohort, let alone people that like Mexican soccer, and a rival.

Seeing this guy with the Chivas backpack made me feel at home, and comfortable enough to joke around. When you are part of the Mexican soccer culture, you're used to hearing jokes and making fun of your rivals. I said, "What are you doing here with that backpack?" He just looked at me, and he laughed, because he understood my joke. Then we just hit it off. In theory, we should dislike each other because our teams are fundamentally polarized. But in reality, we have a lot more in common, such as the profession that we chose, the food that we enjoy, the music that we listen to, and even hobbies that we engage in. We ended up being great friends. This was like a sign from the universe that I was meant to be here, and I knew that it was going to be okay.

Field work

I was raised in a traditional Mexican family. I try to be respectful to the people around me. If you're older than I am, I use the term sir. If you're a lady, I use the term ma'am. That's just who I am. When I was a student, probably two months into level II field work, I remember I had to complete an evaluation, just like any other day. As I was reviewing the patient's chart, I was telling myself to remember all the key details, ask proper questions, and to not forget to establish rapport. That's very important for me because when you're trying to help someone you need their trust, and you need a connection with them. So, I went to greet the lady as she was waiting for me in the lobby. She was pleasant at first, but as soon as we walked into the hallway, right before entering the hand clinic, she said, "Yeah, I don't think I need occupational therapy, I've been here before." I said, "Okay, uh well, let's get this done and then you can fully decline if you don't want therapy." So, we proceeded and she let me complete the evaluation. She had some questions here and there and I was addressing them all. Then, I remember that I used the term ma'am. That's when her demeanor changed. I'm not sure if upset is the right word. She said something along the lines that she wasn't "a ma'am," and to not put her "in a box." I wasn't trying to be harmful. I was trying to be nice, but it did not work with this person because of the one term I used. She looked at me as if I was ignorant or something. She gave me this face. She confused my politeness with bigotry. I learned a lesson, to be patient and professional. We deal with people of all kinds, all walks of life, and it is also our responsibility as therapists to be a little bit extra patient and tolerant.

OT practitioner

I am now a school-based occupational therapist. A lot of our assessments were backed up because of the pandemic and we had a shortage of therapists. I had close to one hundred students and every student had between two and four treatment sessions per month. That's a bunch of treatment sessions. The average number of assessments per school year is around 50, but in my first year I did 83 assessments. I remember sitting in the break room, eating my lunch and there were a few therapists eating with me. They asked how I felt about my caseload. They said, "What do you do to manage the work? Do you take work home?" I explained to them that I felt fine, that I wasn't stressed or anxious. I also mentioned that my work ethic was instilled in me by my parents. My dad worked in the fields for years, picking grapes and onions and carrots. At that time, we lived in Mexico in a border town, so he would cross the border daily. He would wake up every morning at 2am, cross the border to be picked up by 3am, then drive an hour and a half to get to work. He would wait a couple of hours to start his work day. He would start at 6am or 7am and then work for 12 hours. He would drive home, eat dinner, sleep, and do it again, Monday through Friday. He did this for ten years. I grew up with that example. To me that's real work. Not that being an OT practitioner is not real work, we do have a lot of responsibility. However, I don't have to get up in the morning to drive somewhere for two hours and wait there in the cold or the heat; during the summertime it can be 110 or 115 degrees. So, when you have that as a reference, it's hard to complain about anything else.

Introduction

The intention to increase diversity and improve inclusion among the occupational therapy profession has been talked about for some time. An overwhelming number of occupational therapy practitioners and students in the United States (US) identify as white, heterosexual, Christian, and female (American Occupational Therapy Association, 2019). Conversely, the US is racially diverse. This is due in large part to its history of European colonialism, the act of taking over a people and land by force with the outcomes of cultural domination, exploitation for economic gain, and implementation of white supremacy, which is larger than conscious hate. It includes social, political, and economic systems that benefit white majority members over minoritized groups. The US is founded on the European conquest over Native peoples and Native lands to establish settlements with enslaved Africans who were kidnapped to work the settlements for the economic benefit of the European settlers (Abou-Arab & Ashcraft, 2021). Quite clearly, racism is at the root of its foundation. Within the context of historical oppression of socially constructed races, racial and cultural identity (i.e. identities tied to shared cultural experiences) become an integral part of belonging and self-identity (i.e. one's definition and perception of oneself) and an integral part of culture (Abou-Arab & Ashcraft, 2021).

> AOTA affirms the inalienable right of every individual to feel welcomed, valued, a sense of belonging, and respected while accessing and participating in society, regardless of the internal or external

> factors that make every individual unique. (American Occupational
> Therapy Association, 2017, p.1)

Occupational therapy has continued to be a part of these structures that center and prioritize white people and whiteness. Not long ago in 2017, the American Occupational Therapy Association (AOTA) released its Vision 2025 and mission: "Occupational therapy maximizes health, well-being, and quality of life for all people, populations, and communities through effective solutions that facilitate participation in everyday living" (American Occupational Therapy Association, 2017). It created what it called *guideposts*, intended to offer guidance to stakeholders of its *vision*. These were given as *Accessible, Collaborative, Leaders*, and *Effective* (American Occupational Therapy Association, 2017). Nowhere did it specifically or explicitly state the need to improve diversity and it didn't acknowledge the historical or modern implications of racism, prejudice, or discrimination on the people we serve, and our practitioners, students, and other stakeholders. It glossed over generations of trauma and dismissed the journeys of those on the margins. To be clear, it ignored the elephant in the room.

In 2019, AOTA updated Vision 2025 and added a fifth guidepost, entitled *Equity, Inclusion, and Diversity,* urging stakeholders to be "intentionally inclusive and embrace diversity in all its forms" (American Occupational Therapy Association, 2019), a performative piece of jargon at the time with no tangible framework to fulfill this part of its Vision 25. In fact, it wasn't until 2021, a full year after the murder of George Floyd, that AOTA established its Diversity, Equity, and Inclusion Committee. This was a clear reaction to societal pressure, as the demonstrations that followed George Floyd's murder were cited as the largest protest movement in US history (Buchanan *et al.*, 2020). With a profession that is overwhelmingly white, AOTA is guilty of catering to most practitioners who are not directly affected by the systems of white supremacy. To that end, a profession founded by white people continues to center the comfort of white people. This centering and promotion of white experiences as "normal" (without always explicitly naming whiteness, thus using a cultural code) is the comprehensive condition of white supremacy (Gillborn, 2006).

It's important to note that white supremacy systems are not exclusive to discrimination based on race and ethnicity. There has recently been a push to censor education on race and racism in the US at the state level. Simultaneously, there has also been a push for anti-LGBTQIA+ (lesbian, gay, bisexual, transgender, queer, questioning, intersex, and asexual) legislation, highlighting the range of white supremacy (i.e. racism, homophobia, transphobia, and xenophobia). Legislation has been at the forefront in maintaining these systems of power. AOTA has remained consistently silent when it comes to speaking out against these discriminatory policies. Furthermore, the American Occupational Therapy Political Action Committee (AOT-PAC) has directly provided political contributions to politicians who have supported some of the above-mentioned bigoted policies (Open Secrets, 2022). From the founding of our profession until the present day, it has centered whiteness and upheld white supremacy. Occupational therapy is founded on a western Eurocentric lens, dismissing issues of equity, leaving those not a part of the dominant population excluded and on the margins (Iwama, 2007). This limits the stories we hear and learn about, minimizing our collective experiences to a single narrative from a uniform and dominant perspective.

There is a significant risk of harm and danger in looking at our profession, our practitioners, and our students through a singular lens. Chimamanda Adichie, author of *The Danger of the Single Story*, states, "The consequence of the single story is this: It robs people of dignity. It makes our recognition of our equal humanity difficult. It emphasizes how we are different rather than how we are similar."[1] This book intends to de-center whiteness through an *anti-oppression* approach, which refers to the strategies and practices that actively challenge systems of oppression. This work intends to move past what we see as diversity through storytelling. The stories included here intend to move the reader from a singular lens to the multiple

[1] Adapted from *The Danger of a Single Story* [Video], by C.N. Adichie (2009), TED Conferences (www.ted.com/talks/chimamanda_ngozi_adichie_the_danger_of_a_single_story). Copyright 2009, TED Conferences.

perspectives of the minoritized and marginalized groups in occupational therapy; to debunk the often-made mistake in diversity training that perpetuates stereotypes by looking at minority groups as a monolith, or something that is uniform or inflexible. This book continues the shift from *cultural competence* to *cultural humility* and aids in the understanding of the diverse experiences of minoritized occupational therapists in the US.

Each chapter in this book will provide an opportunity to question our biases, stereotypes, and ideology around the human experience. These experiences occur in various practice settings and with a diversity of our clientele throughout the lifespan. These experiences mold the views and interpretations of occupation and the concept of meaningful activities. What is important to one may not be as important to another, and this perspective is essential in providing *client-centered care*. The journeys in this book should deepen our understanding of what it is to not be white, male, Christian, and straight in the field of occupational therapy. It should motivate our profession to engage in meaningful dialogue surrounding social justice matters and to look at the world through these minoritized stories of trauma, resiliency, and triumph. Even in the states where the need for DEI education is acknowledged, most chief diversity officers are white (Brownlee, 2022). So, on the one hand, there are states that are deliberately trying to dismiss the histories of minoritized communities and on the other hand, DEI is being whitewashed and the narratives of the historically oppressed sidelined. This book is much needed in the realm of DEI and occupational therapy, and we hope that the stories will shift thinking and worldviews away from whiteness and the dominant demographic.

Each chapter is about an occupational therapy practitioner who currently practices in the US or completed their training there. They are derived from a semi-structured interview, where they described their journeys into the profession, and reflected on their personal and professional experiences. These chapters are stories of how we came to establish our *occupational identity*, a composite of who we are and wish to be, generated from our histories and experiences (Kielhofner, 2008). This book is not intended as the be-all and end-all of minoritized stories in OT, just the beginning. It merely scratches the surface of the diversity that is among and within us—diversity that needs to be seen and heard. These are our reflections from the margins.

References

Abou-Arab, A. & Ashcraft, R. (2021). Trauma-Informed Care: Historical and Modern Implications of Racism and the Engagement in Meaningful Activities. In A. Lynch, R. Ashcraft, & L. Tekell (eds), *Trauma, Occupation, and Participation: Foundations and Population Considerations in Occupational Therapy* (pp.245–274). Bethesda, MD: AOTA Press.

American Occupational Therapy Association (2017). Vision 2025. *American Journal of Occupational Therapy*, 71(3). Retrieved from: https://doi.org/10.5014/ajot.2017.713002.

American Occupational Therapy Association (2019). AOTA Board Expands Vision 2025. *American Journal of Occupational Therapy*, 73(3). Retrieved from: https://doi.org/10.5014/ajot.2019.733002.

Brownlee, D. (2022). This is Why Corporate DEI Tragically Fails Many Black Professionals. Forbes. August 11. Retrieved from: www.forbes.com/sites/danabrownlee/2022/08/11/this-is-why-corporate-dei-tragically-fails-many-black-professionals/?sh=2a6a2f39efbc.

Buchanan, L., Bui, Q., & Patel, J.K. (2020). Black Lives Matter may be the largest movement in U.S. history. *New York Times*, July 3. Retrieved from: www.nytimes.com/interactive/2020/07/03/us/george-floyd-protests-crowd-size.html.

Gillborn, D. (2006). Rethinking white supremacy: Who counts in 'white world.' *Ethnicities*, 6(3), 318–340. Retrieved from: https://doi.org/10.1177/1468796806068323.

Iwama, M. (2007). Culture and occupational therapy: Meeting the challenge of relevance in a global world. *Occupational Therapy International*, 14(4), 183–187.

Kielhofner, G. (2008). *Model of Human Occupation* (fourth edition). Baltimore, MD: Lippincott, Williams & Wilkins.

Open Secrets (2022). PAC Profile: American Occupational Therapy Association. Retrieved from: www.opensecrets.org/political-action-committees-pacs/american-occupational-therapy-assn/C00089086/summary/2020.

Chapter 1

There's No Part of Me That Desires to be the Outlier

ERICA V. HERRERA

"God bless her, as her memory is waning, she's like, 'What made you get into it?' I said, 'Remember Nana, you are an OT assistant,' and she said, 'Oh yeah, that's right!'" Dana recalls this sweet conversation she had with her grandmother, about her career. Although Dana explains that her grandmother's career choice was not the direct reason she went into occupational therapy, she feels that it may have subconsciously played a role in her decision. "She worked for a state hospital in Kansas for youth with disabilities and did a lot of arts and crafts. So, as I learned in school, I saw where our profession was rooted, even though it shifted to biomechanical." Although Dana's grandmother didn't exactly have the title of occupational therapy assistant (OTA) because this was not an official delineation then, Dana explains, "I'm saying OTA based on how she described herself. She knew that she had an OT who was above her. My grandmother did all of the treatments and then would report to her [the OT]." Dana goes on to share how much her grandmother loved working with "those youths" and loved her profession. Little did Dana know but she would eventually love it too. Dana was born in Georgia but has spent time in Tennessee and Alabama. There is a deep connection to this area as her family has been deeply rooted there for some time. With this connection also lies passion.

> "I self-identify as a Black American Southern woman. I am passionate about my family and passionate about my friends who are my family as well. So, you can often find me pouring into those spaces and spending quality time traveling, usually with a purpose to spend time with all of them. As I've done work in my own doctoral program, I'm learning that as a part of the African American experience, by research, we are very community-based, and so am I."

With this foundation of family, friends, and community, naturally, Dana wanted to enter a career to help people. She majored in health sciences and thought that she would obtain a physical therapy degree; however, she took another route. "I found OT; it was just such a good fit for me. This is because of the way that we look at people. We look at people holistically and I really enjoy the mental health aspect, the physical aspect, and the marriage of those two things." As Dana looks at her own occupations, she recalls, "I love to sing, love nature, love national parks, love quality time, love worship. I am very church and faith oriented as well." Being so spiritually rooted, her next step was to leave the only environment she had ever known and venture out West to start her occupational therapy journey.

Dana's entry into this new environment for graduate school wasn't exactly smooth.

> "Literally my favorite first time to the West Coast story is when I landed to start the program. I couldn't breathe. I was coughing for two weeks and I strongly believe that I wasn't sick. I strongly believe it was because my body had literally never breathed dry air. I am from a region where the air is moist at all times!"

Aside from the physical environment, Dana was very happy to be attending the faith-based program that she wanted. Overall, she felt she had a good experience in OT school. "I found the group that I felt 'did life within the program.' You know, we helped each other out in classes too." When it came to the rigor of academics, Dana felt very supported by those leading her program. However, Dana's personal support had no connections with her academic institution. "I would say personally, I gleaned my support outside the program. I developed a support system off campus, at the church that I joined." This dedication to her faith and overall well-being provided inspiration not only for how she would practice in the future, but the way she wanted to live her life as well. "The part [of the program on the West Coast] that really attracted me went back to faith, spirituality, mental health, and physical health. I felt as if the program encompassed all of that, in a way another program wouldn't."

Nothing in life is perfect. Whether it is a job, house, marriage, or in this case an academic occupational therapy program, there will and should always be room for improvement. Program developers not only need to look at the overall program but also the students who enter the program. By doing so, developers in these academic institutions can better meet the individual needs of the graduate students, on various levels. In a study regarding client satisfaction in OT and rehabilitation, it was noted that "satisfaction refers to the perceived match between expectation and actual circumstances or experiences" (Custer *et al.*, 2015). Being one of two Black American students out of 50 in her cohort, Dana expected to connect more with the other Black student, but she didn't. Dana explains, "I remember, before starting the program, she reached out to say, 'Hey we are here, woohoo!' But to be honest, we started the program and we just never connected in a way that was more than just, 'Hey girl.' It wasn't something intentional but in hindsight, I wish that we had connected more." Dana goes on to express how the relationships that she did develop were those that were formed under "extreme stress" and "doing work" in the program, close together. It is not always the case that we immediately find support, comfort, and solace just because we see someone who looks like us. At the heart of it the shared work, time spent on occupations that are done together, often trumps a connection that is based on appearance alone. When it comes to feeling supported and comfortable in her environment, Dana does in fact prefer a more diverse population of people around her.

"I know there are other African Americans who only like it if it's all African Americans. That's actually not my story. My parents, thank

God for them, were pretty intentional with allowing me to grow up in diverse spaces, meaning Blacks, whites, Hispanics, and Asians. So, I actually feel comfortable in those spaces. I think it's when I'm the only one, or one of two out of 50, that I might get uncomfortable. I try to blend in, as much as I can, and I attribute some of that to my personality. I don't like attention; I don't like to be the center of the room. Unfortunately, you're the automatic center of attention just because you look so different, because you might be the only one. I definitely don't like to be the outlier. I think even when we just think about occupational therapy and social dynamics and group dynamics, I don't know that we are socialized to believe that being the outlier is a good thing. Obviously there are schools of thought that say either 'be the different one' or 'be the change' and all these mantras that we say. But here's the reality: when it comes to social dynamics and group dynamics, you don't want to be the outlier – that's just human nature."

According to the Census, the Black population alone accounts for 13.4% of people in the United States (National Association for the Advancement of Colored People, n.d.). Regardless of whether this population wants the attention or not, the chances are they will be physically noticed in most spaces that they happen to be in. In her graduate program, Dana found herself in this type of situation quite often. People often looked to her for certain cultural answers, as if she were the expert on the topic. "They think I must know about this or that, but what if I actually don't know?" Something that may seem innocent could eventually equate to prolonged pressure. A pressure to be the face and leading example for all those who may look like you, but not actually be like you. A pressure to perform academically, to retrain former ideals of others. Or even a pressure to persuade a group of people to change the environmental norms, so that you can take on the role of who you are, rather than the role you've been selected to play. That's a lot for one or two students out of 50 to handle. That's a lot for a new OT practitioner as they make the transition from the classroom to the workplace.

An occupational therapist's favorite question on earth is: What is occupational therapy? What makes this somewhat comical is that it seems like such a loaded question, especially depending on who you ask. Our title so heavily relies on the first word, occupation. Dana beautifully allows us inside of her picture of occupation as she describes it as "a means to life. It is a means to quality of life. I will even further specify that occupation is like a vehicle to quality of life." For many years, Dana assisted patients in getting into that vehicle and relearning how to control it and how to maneuver it along the most difficult of paths, in order for them to regain independence in their lives. She did this at the most basic level: critical care.

> "Critical care to me, it is really practicing and honing the basics and foundations of occupation. For a lot of patients who are really sick, it sometimes looks like literally lifting their arm. For others, that looks like rolling, for someone else, that looks like sitting up. It could be the difference in being able to lift their arm high enough to brush their teeth with assistance. So, a lot of times in critical care, we're looking at very foundational movements that will lead to occupation."

As occupational therapists, we are put into situations that we may not have been prepared for in school, yet these become our day-to-day interactions and how we care for people.

> "What I love about critical care is that you can find ways to do occupations that you would never think of until you just don't have those means. So, you don't have the strength, or you don't have the cognition, but maybe your eyes are open, and we can use that. We look at different ways to relate very simple movements back to occupation. I think it is very important in critical care because when you're not able to do much you can lose sight of the why, which is the occupation."

It is important that an occupational therapist focuses on what is possible and what someone can do rather than what they cannot do. This is something Dana practices every single day, along with the emotional and mental engagement required to care for her patients at a high and intimate level.

Occupational therapists focus on the words "meaning" and "meaningful activities" when describing the profession. In the book *Spirituality, Health, and Wholeness*, Lamberton and Sorajjakool (2009) talk about meaning in spiritual care as it relates to health, stating that "meaning is an existential journey of the heart. Meaning comes about when one is able to tolerate the irrational turmoil of pain while resting in the embrace of love" (p.89). As occupational beings, we will do and sacrifice anything to hold on to what is meaningful in our lives. One could argue that that is the point of our lives. Not only has Dana worked very closely with reclaiming meaning in her critical care practice, but she has had to take on this experience herself as an OT practitioner.

> "When I see people at their lowest, I am inversely humbled to say 'wow.' Imagine not being able to just reach back and wipe your bottom. As a clinician, it is a humbling experience because I'm watching them really struggle to do something very personal. They can't do it. That's really frustrating and sorrowful, and I'm a stranger and I'm coming in and helping them to do that. It is very humbling, and it is also tough."

The idea of a stranger sharing a very intimate time in a person's life journey during their recovery process may seem distant and cold for the patient but in fact, this is why hospitals were created. Lamberton and Sorajjakool (2009, p.89) remind us that the word *hospital* derives from *hospis*, which means both "stranger" and "host", and *pito* meaning "lord" or "powerful one". "The hospital is a place where the stranger can find rest, protection, and care." Whether it is the giving or receiving of care, people may start off as strangers, but by way of the environment and the sense of meaning, both patient and clinician can assist in the patient process in creating the needed tools to return to occupation and meaningful activities. Unfortunately, at times, that process can place a burden on the clinician.

At one of the most top-rated hospitals in the US, Dana is not only exceptionally trained for her position as a critical care OT practitioner but she also leads by example and holds herself to a high standard of patient care. This includes building the rapport and relationships needed for a rehabilitative outcome that is satisfactory for the patient and Dana, the therapist. She acknowledges some of the details of care:

> "When they're critically ill, you become family — you kind of have to. Connecting is a bonding activity for those who allow it. Certainly, you have those who are, for their own reason, resistant. I think when you're in a very vulnerable position with people at their lowest, most of the time, you connect and bond with them quickly."

In such a severe state of illness, you might think that you would be seeking the aid of a skilled professional with the utmost care but clearly this is not always the case.

> "I think the most egregious example that I can remember is when a patient literally asked to have a white therapist. Literally. I had a Caucasian student with me, and we both went into the room. What the patient didn't know was that the Caucasian therapist she was referring to was a student and didn't know how to treat her. The patient was adamantly saying, 'I want you to leave, and I want her to stay.' And so, bearing in mind patient autonomy and patient choice, whatever the case may be, the patient was cognitive enough to consent, and so I had to leave the room and figure out a way to rescue my student!"

This situation was not just difficult for Dana but also challenging for the student. Dana is grateful that she has learned the skills to modify, adapt, and, most importantly, build trust quickly. "Just with the human and patient interaction, if you get off on the wrong foot, often it's really hard to get back into gear, especially if there's already a bias there." Some of the disconnection is due to the nature of Dana's specialty, but much of it is due to how she is viewed just because of what she looks like. In OT, there is power in therapeutic use of self, as

Dana has depicted. Often, this (in a positive way) overshadows other skilled interventions we may implement. However, when you are a person of color or the "outlier" as Dana has shared, the legs of your therapeutic self may be cut before you even start. Dana described the "undertones of dislike" that patients have verbalized, such as "Is somebody coming with you?" or "Oh, do you have a partner?" or "Is it really you, where's your badge?"

Despite this, Dana adores her job and being an OT practitioner in critical care. However, she does not disagree that the extra work from this focus is exhausting. In her book *Medical Apartheid*, Harriet Washington (2006) explores in detail the many experimental scientific and medical procedures on slaves and modern-day Blacks. She discusses how doctors used slaves to perform many experimental caesarean sections, bladder stone removals, and ovariectomies. Slaves were used because it was thought that "Blacks did not feel pain or anxiety." Harriet further writes that this "excused painful surgical explorations without anesthesia on Blacks" (p.58). If this was the thought process in the mid 1800s, have we eradicated it or fed it into more systems than we know? Dana has definitely felt this utter disregard in her own practice.

> "When I say that I am being overlooked or being underestimated, I know that from first-hand experience. I walk into a room, for example, with my Caucasian physical therapy partner and the patient literally doesn't acknowledge me or they don't look at me, or they think I'm a tech or whatever the case may be. It is just exhausting; I have to fight to build trust. It really comes down to even micro things that you do, like the way that you walk into the room, the way that you introduce yourself, how you look at the patient and also acknowledge their family. Some of those things I have to pick up on intuitively because you have a very short amount of time. When I walk into the room I have maybe ten seconds to establish all of that, but it takes 0.3 seconds to see that I am African American."

On a larger scale, Dana reflects on the entire African American community:

"I definitely think that African Americans are significantly at an increased risk of burnout because we are managing so many other dynamics that our counterparts do not have to. I believe that leads us to burnout quicker because there are just so many layers to what we do."

As we know, as human beings, there are so many layers to us all, aside from race itself. The author of *Black Pain*, Terrie M. Williams (2008), reminds us that "the outer layer of people's lives never shows us how many holes the person has inside" (p.xxviii). Dana loves occupational therapy and all that it stands for but says, "instead of feeling like you have to do the theatrics, sometimes you want to show up and just be." As occupational therapists, we have so much power to change, to influence, and to really attack the need where it stands. Sometimes this need is not something we can see, but is much greater. As we learn and grow in our skills, we must do the same with our thoughts and emotions; not just for those we serve but for ourselves.

"I believe that I have a personal responsibility to be a good represen- tation, by God's grace, of what it looks like to be an African American practitioner. It is possible for humans to think one way about you, maybe because of the color of your skin, but actually change their mind after a positive experience. An experience with someone who's different can go really well just due to basic human kindness. We're in this together. I can think of times when I believe that the person not only left the hospital stronger from an OT standpoint, but also from a humanistic standpoint, knowing that they made it through with the help of someone who looked nothing like them. Honestly prior to this, I never would have thought that I could even be eligible to help them. It takes being at your lowest, really, to understand that these barriers that we have that we set up in our mind, whether it be because of upbringing or where we grew up, don't have to be barriers. We can just allow them to fall. This dismantling of barriers will take a while, but I do think as OTs we have a role in that, because of how holistically we are trained and how holistically we speak. I venture to say that we should be at the top of the list of professionals who are committed to being examples of this. There are lots of professional groups who talk about it, who are about it, but we can be it because of who we are."

REFLECTION QUESTIONS

1. How would you respond if a client refuses to "work" with you because of your race/ethnicity? What steps might you take to address the situation?
2. Reflect on your therapeutic use of self. How do you utilize it in practice to build rapport and connect with your clients on a humanistic level?
3. What strategies can be developed to increase awareness of unconscious and implicit bias so that practitioners are able to intentionally implement these resources/tools in their practice setting?

References

Custer, M., Huebner, R., & Howell, D. (2015). Factors predicting client satisfaction in occupational therapy and rehabilitation. *American Journal of Occupational Therapy*, 69(1), 6901290040.

Lamberton, H. & Sorajjakool, S. (2009). *Spirituality, Health, and Wholeness: An Introductory Guide for Health Care Professionals*. London: Routledge.

National Association for the Advancement of Colored People (NAACP) (n.d.). Criminal Justice Fact Sheet. Retrieved from: https://naacp.org/resources/criminal-justice-fact-sheet.

Washington, H. (2006). *Medical Apartheid*. New York, NY: DoubleDay Publishing.

Williams, T. (2008). *Black Pain: It Just Looks Like We Are Not Hurting*. New York, NY: Scribner.

Chapter 2

An Onus on Justice

ALAA ABOU-ARAB

British colonization reaches far and wide, and its history is horrid. In the early 20th century, at the height of its dominance, the British Empire ruled over a quarter of the earth's land, and from 1860, ships took hundreds of Indian people from India to South Africa (both countries were British colonies at the time) to develop the sugar industry as indentured workers. The majority of Indian South Africans are the descendants of these people who were brought to South Africa between 1860 and 1911 (South African History Online, 2022). This is Ushentha's story. "I am culturally Indian; I am a fourth generation South African Indian, a product of colonialism, I am a part of the Indian diaspora." The Indian diaspora as a result of British colonization can be found all over the globe, but in South Africa it was even more oppressive.

> "I was born at a point where apartheid was still practiced in South Africa. Laws of separation, segregation, racism, were fully enforced when I was a child. Those ideas of being othered, subjugated, the recipe of prejudice and racism are things that I understand."

Ushentha moved to the US with her family when she was 16 years old. Some of what she witnessed as a child in South Africa waited for her in a new land. She fully understood and felt the idea of being othered. It resonates with her when she sees these things practiced time and again. "It angers me and it's something that, as a result of my upbringing, I feel strongly about." It's important to understand that the practice of apartheid is a tool used to maintain white supremacy, but it isn't the only way it's maintained. Ushentha has been a witness to how white supremacy has been practiced in a variety of ways, with its goal of maintaining the dominance that was created by the initial takeover and colonization. That systemic injustice carried from generation to generation, from colony to colony, is what motivates Ushentha to fight forward. "Even in New Jersey, which has a very diverse population, but within healthcare and certainly within our profession, finding safe spaces to have conversations like this has been challenging...but I feel it's my personal responsibility to address social injustice."

You wouldn't assume that a person of color, a product of colonialism and apartheid, would decide to pursue a career that is over 80% white in the US. We all have our journey leading to entering the profession. Ushentha's journey began by completing high school in New York state and going on to get her bachelor's degree in psychology. Her father is a physician and her mother a social worker, so she always had something of a healthcare context. "Being surrounded by healthcare workers, the conversations at the dinner table, it was a familiar realm for me." Despite the proximity to healthcare, she had not heard of OT. It wasn't until she got a job working with adults with developmental disabilities that she discovered OT and began to see the scope of what was available. Occupational therapy practitioners can work with individuals across the lifespan and in a plethora of settings, in homes, schools, hospitals, and clinics. She then decided to pursue a master's in OT and attended a university in New York.

She recalls her experience in OT school: "There were approximately 80 students in my OT class, and I was one of three individuals who classified themselves as South Asian: two females and one male." Ushentha quickly felt that she was being othered; with only two females of Indian origin, classmates and faculty staff often mistakenly took one for the other. Microaggressions like these are common throughout this text, but they are not micro in the sense of the trauma inflicted. "They are commonplace daily verbal, behavioral, or environmental indignities, whether intentional or unintentional, that communicate hostile, derogatory, or negative racial slights and insults towards people of color" (Sue *et al.*, 2007, p.271). More importantly, these daily occurrences pile onto each other, further adding to the trauma of these lived experiences. Frankly, microaggressions are not *micro* whatsoever and often occur even if the offending individual is unaware of the consequences of their actions.

A common theme in many of the stories collected in this book is of these individuals having to carry the burden of representing everyone—in this case, the Indian diaspora. "It's an everyday occurrence, with a name like Ushentha. I have to say my name several times to everybody. Yes, I am Indian, but I am South African, I was always painting the path for myself every day." It is crucial for OT students and practitioners to understand that the intent of their words or actions does not absolve them from the potential effects of those words and actions. Simply put, if you walk into a closed door unintentionally, it will still hurt you. If you walk into that closed door repeatedly, over and over again, it will hurt you more.

Although not as common as it used to be, the concept of cultural competency was popular at the time of Ushentha's OT training, with the college holding various cultural events. In terms of the time spent talking about issues involving diversity, equity, or inclusion in the classroom, Ushentha states, "When I think of the curriculum, it was not a discussion... My entire faculty was white or looked white to me." While often well intended, cultural events such as potlucks can further marginalize non-white Christian people in these settings. This can place stress on these students to present their ethnic and cultural background, because there is a pressure to perform. Ushentha was one of just a few people from the Indian diaspora in her classroom, with an all-white faculty, while trying to meet the demands of the coursework. Seeking support was a challenge, and one she continued to encounter as she entered the workplace.

"When I got my first job, it became more apparent to me how the culture around me was white centric, I had to learn to navigate this... and this was in New York City. In graduate school, you get to kind of choose who you socialize with, whereas in the work environment, the culture is thrust upon you. You must figure out how to integrate and how to speak the language. I've learned because of my lived experiences, what to say and what not to say and how to make people feel comfortable."

Her first job out of school was in a major hospital that had multiple services such as acute care, and inpatient and outpatient rehabilitation; she worked in the inpatient unit. In school, she learned of occupation as an individual's ability to achieve success. Now as a practitioner, both her personal and professional experiences gave her an expertise in navigating difficult and marginalizing situations. Non-white occupational therapists can struggle with trying to build a rapport with patients and clients when the patient is distracted by or curious about their ethnic background. A non-white woman in what Ushentha refers to as a "white-centric" workplace has to navigate barriers she has no control over. "Can I relate to your American values? That was my everyday thing and, honestly, I became very good as a result of trying to prove myself every day. I was very good at what I did."

She became a great OT, relishing moments with patients as they met goals. "I did everything I needed to do to demonstrate my abilities. I climbed the clinical ladder; I checked all the boxes." She worked hard, looking to advance her career and the profession. She had been with the same organization for over ten years and was ready for the next challenge. A promotion became available and Ushentha felt as though she'd done enough to earn it. "They had to acknowledge that I could do it all." She was offered the position and has been working on the administrative and managerial side since then. This validation is not something that Ushentha takes for granted. In systems that were not built for her to succeed, achieving the promotion is a triumph. However, the day-to-day othering and microaggressions continue. Now, she recognizes the harmful rhetoric, even though it isn't directed at her. The knowledge base of marginalized experiences can make one privy to how words and actions coming from the dominant group may be perceived. "Things rub me the wrong way and it's normally never directed at me...it's unsettling because you're approached as though you agree. Then I must be polite or ignore it because that is what we do in hospital systems...that has happened numerous times."

Her views on occupation have also changed since moving away from patient care. When asked what her favorite occupation was, she recollects those moments with patients. "My favorite occupation used to be that moment with a patient where you know you made a change that was significant to them." OTs from everywhere—and those included in this book—have echoed this sentiment. She sees occupation now through a wider lens. "In these last years, my idea of occupation has shifted to a more global idea, not just individuals, but communities being impacted by a lack of access due to politics, socioeconomics, you name it... I've grown and it's interesting to see that change."

Following the murder of George Floyd, many occupational therapy organizations began to initiate diversity, equity, and inclusion initiatives. With her position in leadership, Ushentha had an interesting perspective. She noted the sense of urgency at the time for the organization to do what was right. "They are definitely taking it seriously now, but it's all very grassroots and it's yet to be determined what's going to happen." People of color in leadership positions have talked about the pressures put on them in 2020 to be a voice, expert, or organizer. Women of color activists had gender and cultural expectations of selflessness, and the cumulative impact on multiple minoritized identities increased the risk for burnout. Organizations, universities, and hospital systems offered what was considered to be a safe space. Listening sessions and panels filled with stories of the marginalized, often dismissing much of what they might have been through or triggers that might arise. Ushentha experienced it differently: "I honestly think the best experiences for me as a professional have been in these DEI initiatives." She decided to further her love for OT and DEI work, and achieved a doctorate in occupational therapy, with her research focusing on the experiences of women of color in OT.

"The title of my research project was 'Leadership Development of

Women of Color in Occupational Therapy in the US: A Qualitative Intersectional Analysis.' I explored the intersectional experience of eight women of color leaders in OT, looking closely at how their overlapping social identities affected their leadership development. The participants' predominant intersecting patterns converged into four themes: early leadership development does not happen without access to opportunities; sponsorship and mentorship have consequences beyond one's leadership development; being seen is essential for leadership development; and persevering is a constant state of struggle. The four central themes illustrate how leadership development for women of color in OT rests at the intersection of scholarship, mentorship, and authentic inclusion. Future action in OT must include mentorship and sponsorship models and programs to support professionals of color in OT."

She now feels less othered, less marginalized, and more powerful. Her journey spans the globe, from British colonization to apartheid South Africa and the constant microaggressions experienced in her career. She found achievements through a justice-based lens. She has found community in some of the values she's always believed in. As we collectively strive for a more inclusive and equitable profession, we're grateful to have Ushentha, a colleague who places the onus on justice.

REFLECTION QUESTIONS

1. Have you ever been pulled into culturally inappropriate conversations? How did you or could you have handled it?
2. Have you been witness to discrimination or prejudice as a bystander? What did you do? What should you have done?

References

Indian South Africa (2022). South African History Online: Towards a People's History. Retrieved from: www.sahistory.org.za/article/indian-south-africans#:~:text=The%20first%20Indians%20arrived%20during,of%20the%20slaves%20were%20Indians.

Sue, D.W., Capodilupo, C.M., Torino, G.C., Bucceri, J.M., *et al.* (2007). Racial microaggressions in everyday life. *American Psychologist*, 62(4), 271–286. doi: 10.1037/0003-066X.62.4.271.

Chapter 3

Amalgamate

ERICA V. HERRERA

Amalgamate can be defined in a few different ways. The most comprehensible explanation is to connect or unify two or more objects (Merriam-Webster, 2022b). This could be a myriad of components, however, such as an organization, people, cultures, objects, or even metals. Although this coming together is foundationally the same, it is interesting to visualize the comparison between cultures and metal. Let's take metal, for instance. The amalgamation process takes a natural rock called an ore and attempts to extract the valuable mineral, such as gold or silver, that is contained within it. However, in order to do this, the ore has to be ground up and mixed with mercury to create the amalgam. This amalgam is not ore, not mercury, but something else. It is this "something else" that gets heated to completely dissolve the mercury. All that is left is a valuable mineral, such as gold. Understanding amalgamation in culture is very similar in the sense that the end result is "something else."

The connections that are built from the many transactions are no longer owned by one side or the other because it is something that was created that is new. There is separation between acculturation or colonisation (changing a culture's beliefs through conquest) and assimilation (one of the cultural groups takes on the ways of doing from the other) from amalgamation (Merriam-Webster, 2022a, 2022d, 2022c). Throughout history, we have definitely done the former and continue to do so today. An argument could be made that the best of the three would be amalgamation. There is no one element or culture that prevails or completely has to adopt the other, but something more valuable, more beautiful, comes from the exchange.

Alice takes us through her amalgamation process as a young first-generation Korean American woman.

> "I am Alice, Korean. I was born in Southern California and I have been here my whole life. I've grown up around Asians my whole life; that's kind of all I knew. I didn't really know any other cultural backgrounds; I was in my own bubble."

Regardless of this particular start in life being perceived as good or bad, it definitely provided her with a very innocent and hopeful view of the world she would enter.

Growing up in a tight-knit, secluded environment can often lead to someone taking a similar path to that others in the same environment have been on. However, Alice felt comfortable branching out. Perhaps it was the lack of marginalization in her world that led to this fearless and willing attitude to do anything and everything. She explains, "I definitely wanted to help people in some kind of way, but it was hard to fine-tune how. There are so many different options [to help] we don't even know exist." Alice later found out that the three people she looked up to and aspired to be like, at church, were all occupational therapists. If you believe in fate or destiny, this would be a prime example. The world of occupational therapy is not large in comparison to other professions. In 2018, the Health Resources and Services Administration reported the number of occupational therapists in the US to be roughly 104,000 practitioners, which is significantly less than physical therapists, estimated at 237,000, and respiratory therapists at 111,000 practitioners (U.S. Department of Health and Human Services, 2018). To have three occupational therapists at the same church who are also family friends is nothing short of a miracle. After Alice spoke with her family friends and learned how to enter the profession, she decided to attend California State University of Fullerton as a psychology major, in order to prepare for her occupational therapy path. Now, this is where it gets interesting.

Alice joyfully explains how she had really good family support during her undergraduate studies. This support, however, did not consider her parents' reluctance toward the major she chose. My parents said "'Psychology Why would you that? What do you do with psychology?'" Alice clarifies, "[my parents] don't believe in psychology; this is very common in Korean culture. They don't believe in going to therapy of any kind. They don't buy into any of that. They just believe in medicine." This question regarding psychology is interesting, considering how occupational therapy got started. In the book *The Making of Rehabilitation*, Glitzer and Arluke (1985) note that the roots of occupational therapy are linked to Egyptian practices, which found the connection between activity and recovery from illness. This then led to practices in European asylums, where there were improvements in both physical and mental conditions. Dr. William Rush Dunton Jr., who is considered to be the "father of OT," saw first-hand how occupational therapy practices led to the recovery of his psychiatric patients. Although the importance of medicine is indisputable, one of the best advancements in medicine is the discovery of allied health professions, such as occupational therapy.

As practitioners, we want to serve our populations to the best of our ability, but how can we do that if we do not look in-depth at what each culture believes to be important or unimportant regarding their health? In 2018, Jang and colleagues conducted a study that looked at the willingness of Korean Americans to use counseling services, as well as what their roles and beliefs were regarding depression. They found that in most Asian cultures, people believe that issues of the mind are a result of a person's inability to control their emotions. The individual also does not want to speak of mental ill-health in fear of bringing shame to their family. Specifically, in Korean culture, the study also discovered that health is considered physical health only and that suppression of psychological issues is a virtue to be revered, as an example of good self-control (Jang *et al.*, 2018). How does an occupational therapist navigate these differences? Anne Wilson Schaef, author of the book *Native Wisdom for White Minds*, writes, "To understand the belief system in which I live, it helps to have the perspective of another system" (1995, July 5). Although Alice comes from a foundational system, a culture and world that has very alternative views to that of western culture, she still finds herself drawn to explore these new ways.

After Alice was accepted on to the occupational therapy program, she continued living with her parents as she did in her undergraduate studies, and commuted to the university. She explains the difference by stating, "I didn't feel like undergraduate when I commuted, as I didn't really have friends there; I just went and left. At least in the occupational therapy program we were together all day. We became really close and supported each other all the way." Being on the introverted side, Alice naturally gravitated to a group that was like her in ways that felt familiar and comfortable. She described her group as being similar in age, with familiar family dynamics, and also Asian. On reflection, Alice is not surprised that her group of friends comprised all the Korean students in the class. Alice further reminds us that "you naturally start migrating towards people who are 'your own kind,' especially when they are strangers; it's easier to understand each other." This is very true for many of us. There is an ease of connection when there are already identifiable traits that may be in common. Most of the time, what we see visually can lead us to the next steps of starting or avoiding a new interaction. However, over time, there are also other connections that can grow or cease regardless of outward appearance, but more focused on the spirit of an individual. Although Alice may have naturally gravitated toward people who looked like her while in the occupational therapy program, she developed a strength for seeing people through a spiritual lens.

During Alice's time as an occupational therapy student, this spiritual lens allowed her to see people for who they were. In reference to her professors, Alice says, "I feel as if I had so many different role models I looked up to but all of them were very different from me." Although she was aware of these differences, it never bothered her. Instead, she found beauty in it. She expresses this by stating, "The really fascinating thing about OT [practitioners] in general is that I've never really met anyone who was very similar; everyone is so unique and different. They all have a different story, a different mission, and a different passion." Alice saw this as a strength. She was entering an inimitable profession which encompassed a versatility of people and views. Although she is very proud of the choice she made, not all memories are fond ones.

Alice had the opportunity to volunteer at an occupational therapy clinic while she was a student. She recalls that the occupational therapist was wonderful, but the lead volunteer seemed to like everyone but her. Alice never knew why he felt this way. The lead volunteer's behavior toward Alice started to interfere with her time at the volunteer site. Alice recalls, "One day I just couldn't take it anymore. I felt so suffocated every time I was on my way to that place because of that one guy." To her surprise, he finally addressed her, "There was one day, where he basically revealed why he didn't like me. He said, 'I don't like Koreans. You guys just have a really small standard of beauty.' I was amazed." Although he was not Korean, he was also of Asian descent. Alice was surprised that he wouldn't ask about his concerns prior to judging her solely based on the race she happens to belong to. After the incident, she recalls, "I almost wanted to quit. I could have quit at that point because I had way too many volunteer hours but I really liked that place." How many people have had to sacrifice their dreams, places of employment, living environment, or educational endeavors because of incidents like Alice's? Just escape it and it will be better somewhere else—but will it?

Given that she had not had a racial experience before, Alice handled herself as a professional. She sought the assistance of her supervising OT practitioner to try and have a facilitated discussion on how to move forward. She did find more peace in knowing why the lead volunteer was treating her differently as opposed to the information never being divulged. Being upfront, as the lead volunteer had been, was at least a step in the right direction. In 2006, Czopp and colleagues found that the confrontation may reduce future biased responses regarding race (Czopp *et al.*, 2006). One could argue that even the most difficult situations, such as prejudices or racial issues, are still better handled when brought to light.

As much of a "bubble," sheltered around Asians, as Alice's upbringing was, it is ironic that the first person to show racial disdain toward her was also Asian.

"I really never had a job before being an OT [practitioner]. I wasn't smart, just book smart." As an OT practitioner, Alice has had a myriad of experiences that have enriched her life and also the lives of her patients. Alice does still find comfort in treating other Asians because of the "easy" connections but is proud to say that many of her clinical experiences are with people of other races, backgrounds, and cultures. She states:

> "You think as a therapist that you are the one helping people but from talking to so many different kinds of people, they are actually helping you. I think nowadays, with how the world is going, it is easy to think more pessimistically and badly about people. However, when you actually are forced to be face-to-face with a person that you never would have had the opportunity to talk to, you realize that person is pretty amazing! I've had that experience 99% of the time with my patients. If it weren't for the work that I do as an OT practitioner, I probably would not have ever come to that conclusion."

Every day, Alice is creating "something new" with her patients, mixing the foundations of who she is as a Korean woman along with her occupational therapy education. She is able to create the spiritual lens needed to see inside people and build that connection we all desperately need—especially when we are trying to heal.

REFLECTION QUESTIONS

1. Alice stated that we naturally gravitate toward people who are our own kind. How can this help or hinder patient care as an OT?
2. Were you surprised that Alice's first experience of direct discrimination came from another person of Asian descent? Did you assume it was a white person? If so, why did you have that assumption?

3. Have you ever almost quit something because of harassment or discrimination, even if you loved it? If you stayed, why was that?

4. Would it help you or frighten you if a patient, colleague, or professor was direct in their feelings toward an unchangeable characteristic of yours?

References

Acculturation. (2022a). Merriam-Webster.com. Retrieved from: www.merriam-webster.com/dictionary/acculturation.

Amalgamate. (2022b). Merriam-Webster.com. Retrieved from: www.merriam-webster.com/dictionary/amalgamate.

Assimilation. (2022c). Merriam-Webster.com. Retrieved from: www.merriam-webster.com/dictionary/assimilation.

Colonization. (2022d). Merriam-Webster.com. Retrieved from: www.merriam-webster.com/dictionary/colonization.

Czopp, A.M., Monteith, M.J., & Mark, A.Y. (2006). Standing up for a change: Reducing bias through interpersonal confrontation. *Journal of Personality and Social Psychology*, 90(5), 784–803.

Glitzer, G. & Arluke, A. (1985). *The Making of Rehabilitation*. Los Angeles, CA: University of California Press.

Jang, Y., Yoon, H., Park, N.S., Rhee, M., & Chiriboga, D.A. (2018). Mental health service use and perceived unmet needs for mental health care in Asian Americans. *Community Mental Health Journal*, 55, 241–248.

Schaef, A.W. (1995). *Native Wisdom for White Minds: Daily Reflections Inspired by the Native Peoples of the World*. New York, NY: Ballantine Books.

U.S. Department of Health and Human Services, Health Resources and Services Administration (2018). *The U.S. Health Workforce Chartbook. Part IV: Behavorial and Allied Health*. Rockville, MD: U.S. Department of Health and Human Services.

Chapter 4

No, I Was Not Surprised

ERICA V. HERRERA

Being the youngest child in the family can come with many perks. As Tenika proudly explains, "I didn't want for anything; I had everything that I needed." She laughingly elaborates, stating, "As the baby of the family, I still get a lot of my wants [fulfilled] as an adult." However, Tenika's upbringing was not without hard work and challenges. The youngest of three siblings in her family, and granddaughter to a line of educated professionals, there was a high expectation of greatness in her home. To further paint this picture, Tenika emphasizes that her brother has a bachelor's degree in computer science, her sister has a degree as a nursing assistant, her father worked as an educator, and both Tenika's mother and grandmother were working on their bachelor's degrees at the same time! "A lot of my experiences have been tapered and tailored by my family's expectations that were placed on me," Tenika says. For this reason, Tenika's academic success included challenges stemming largely from the environment of her upbringing.

In reference to the Tuskegee shirt worn at the time of the interview, Tenika explains, "I did not go to Tuskegee, I teach at Tuskegee. My college is Alabama State University, and they are rivals with Tuskegee. So, oh, it is a big deal down here in the South." Tenika speaks with pure joy as she converses about the different Southern schools, their rivalries, and what it is like to be in that prideful atmosphere in the South. However, others from this region of the country, including some members of Tenika's family, have had different experiences in the education system.

> "My mom was a part of the integration process and was one of the first Black students to attend Lee High School here in Montgomery. There were only six Black students at the high school when she went and, you know, she told me different things."

Many parents may reflect on things they want to be sure to teach their children, such as not to run in the street, to make sure to respectfully ask adults rather than tell them when you need something, or even make sure to wash your hands when entering different locations. This is nowhere near the same level of "things" Tenika was told. Tenika recalls these "things" to be racial slurs and race relations in the South that were shared with her from her mother's experience. Tenika was very clear about how this impacted her.

> "A lot of those things that she told me and some of the experiences that she shared with me have definitely shaped my view and my outlook. I wouldn't ever want myself or my child – or anyone – to be subjected to that. So I just had the drive to do better because it was required."

Tenika did not feel she had the option to do anything else but be "better." Although her competitive nature has led her to do better than "better," one shouldn't have to feel forced into their purpose out of fear of not being supported by their environment. The strength that Tenika possesses has been her greatest gift and her Achilles' heel.

Many OT practitioners have unique stories of how they came to become an OT. Some will refer to the time their grandparent had a stroke, and the OT was the one who assisted them in regaining their independence. Others may talk of a personal experience they had with an injury and the OT guided them in their meaningful activities and to regain what they had loved to do prior to their injury. There are even some who were volunteering under another discipline but happened to gravitate toward the OT as they were jumping on a trampoline with a child to work on vestibular skills and motor planning. But for Tenika, "I needed to do something different, but it was really my friend's suggestion. She thought I'd be a great OT and that I should look into it." During this time, Tenika was excelling in the university system in her home state. She was on a path to respiratory therapy and felt it came naturally to her. "I was rocking those respiratory classes! Boom, boom, boom! I didn't need to go to study sessions, I worked on my own and I was used to that." Although she was completing her tasks at a very high level, a certain professor did not see it that way. "One of my clinical instructors accused me of completing a 'check-off' on a clinical task but said I didn't actually do it. She said I just put it into the system." This situation happened well over two decades ago, yet Tenika recalls it as if it were yesterday. "Other people saw me put the information in, right, but to her I was this little Black girl. I could've stayed but I ended up leaving that school." This would be the beginning of various support system issues that Tenika faced when trying to complete her education. "I didn't feel welcomed, I didn't feel wanted, I didn't feel respected," she says. If you are in a collegiate environment with thousands of students and staff, yet you feel that you are in it by yourself, how are you expected to succeed?

Tenika went on to transfer to a historically Black college or university (HBCU) to embark on her OT journey. "I had a full scholarship to pay for tuition and books, so it was pleasant for the month." Unfortunately, the treatment and lack of support she experienced regarding her educational path was not much different from how it had been at the college she previously attended. Regarding the pleasantness of her time in the new college, Tenika states, "It was my friends, not the program." Tenika does recall good experiences with her clinical instructors (there was one particular white professor whom she learned the most from), but the support was still not there. There was only one Black professor. For people who may not be familiar with the experience at HBCUs, it is common to assume that when you think of an HBCU, you think of Black students and staff everywhere! Unfortunately, the only Black professor Tenika had was not a source of support during her OT program. "He told me my ponytail was not professional and that I should consider changing it." Tenika had proudly joined a sorority, to which she attributes much of her educational success because of the deep relationships she made. They had an event on campus and presented a signature hairstyle for the event. "White girls wear their hair in really long ponytails, why don't you tell them that they are not professional? Why is my ponytail not professional? Do you understand what I'm saying? It's the same hair style!"

Despite the scant support from her Caucasian faculty, and none from the only Black faculty member, Tenika still managed to complete her program. What was it within her that got her through?

> "You know if you catch me on the right day, you probably will have no idea that I have a doctorate. I can shine it up and clean it up for you and be just as articulate and you'll never have a clue. That grit within me that is so genuine to who I am, it's never going to go anywhere. I can't erase it. I am from the west side of Montgomery. I can't get rid of it...so you know, I think that's what they were picking up on. I think that's what everybody picks up on. The real genuineness of It all, I just can't erase, and I really don't want to. I like me."

As a professor now, Tenika tries to be the professor she wished she had. She describes how she tries to utilize real life examples in her courses in order to impact the learning process. "I'm doing 30-minute office hours sessions and I'm telling them how to study and organize their notes." This is an experience Tenika felt that she did missed out on. Being able to communicate with her professors was not just an issue for her but for many of her cohort. "We started with 15 students in the program. Two were white and the rest Black. When I graduated, there were six Black [students] and two white." When asked about the possible reasons for this, Tenika cites many examples but one in particular pertaining to office hours.

> "Certain students in the class would always pass, but they never knew the right answers when we were in study groups, and they could never answer the questions in class because they never knew

the answer. When it was time to test they always did well and when we would try to go in the office they were always in the professor's office. The professors would tell us *we* were unprepared for office hours."

Tenika further explains, "It's office hours, so you are supposed to go in and ask questions for clarification." Tenika says she would ask for help and be turned away because of unpreparedness once again. So, she says, "I never made another appointment, I never did." If this was the foundation of her program, it is not surprising that other students of color could not make it through. Everyone has their own circumstances and set of challenges during academic course work, but the support and nurturing that come from the educating professional in the field you are entering are vital for success. Tenika can attest to this need for support, especially because these early experiences shaped her as a clinician and professor.

Tenika practiced clinically for years before obtaining her doctorate degree. When she embarked on this new journey to re-enter the collegiate system, she brought prior experiences with her. She candidly states, "I was a seasoned professional by the time I got to the doctorate program. I had been the only Black clinician in 90% of the jobs that I had before, so I already knew how to move in those circles." For Tenika, this was not something she wanted to be good at because, she explains, "I kind of clung to those who wanted to be around me whether they looked like me or not, you know, because I have friends from all different types of nationalities. I'm drawn to energy." Unfortunately, as a survival technique in the university system, she learned how to navigate in order to accomplish what she needed to.

"There is a fear of the judgment that's going to come as soon as I open my mouth. As soon as I ask my question, there's a fear of not being good enough. I can say that when I got there, the first semester, I was much more closed off but by the time I graduated I had opened up more."

As Tenika ventured into various practice settings in different states and completed her doctorate program in a different state, her perspective started to change and mature in a way that reflected more of who she really was rather than who she had to adapt to be.

> "Not everybody is judgmental, not everybody feels that way, not everybody was raised in an environment where Black people were belittled, where they were looked down on and seen as less than. That mindset has caused me to lose some opportunities for growth and for professional development. So that is crippling because now being Dr. Danley, I am looking for those opportunities, I want those opportunities."

Thankfully for Tenika, she has been able to reflect and implement changes for growth. Can you and I say the same or are we, too, missing our opportunities? She makes these opportunities, but it can be very challenging and at times, even racist. Tenika was flying back home from attending her doctoral program and having a conversation with her classmate and the person seated behind her. They were conversing about projects for school. Coincidentally, the person seated next to Tenika chimed in, "Are you an OT?" Tenika went on to tell the person about her OTD program and about her career. Then another person on the plane blurted out, "My son is an OT."

> "There was just a whole family of OTs on the plane! Her husband asked me, 'So you're from Alabama, right?' I said, 'Yeah.' He said, 'So did you grow up in the projects?' I said, 'Excuse me?' He said, 'I've just never heard a Black person as articulate as you are.' I was on the plane, and I looked at my classmate, and she was just looking like...'I don't know what to say.' Long story short, we got to the airport, and I couldn't stay in the airport and sit next to this man. I had to go outside and breathe, and it was snowing outside but I had to get out, I needed that cold air, I needed it, Lord. The West side of me was thinking, 'I wanted to hit this man' but I couldn't, because the professional in me was saying, 'You're going to go to jail.' The Black woman in me was saying, 'You're going to go to jail if you hit this white man in the airport, okay!' So, I knew that but it was just very offensive. Did I grow

up in the projects?! Then he tells me that he has never seen a Black person as articulate as me?! I'm not even the best I know; there are way more Black people who are more articulate than I am, on a good day! It's things like that that I feel white people will never understand. To have your character and your value questioned, you know? Really, why would you ask me that? What is it that I said that you heard, that made you feel you wanted to ask me if I grew up in the projects?"

After completion of her OT degree, Tenika worked in New York for two years and then in Alabama for the rest of her clinical years. Considering that New York and Alabama are two very different environments, Tenika explains, "I did my 12 weeks [of field work in OT school in New York] there so that is how I got introduced to it." Of all the places Tenika has worked, she reflects on the fact that she was always the only person of color, except while in New York. When talking about this school-based setting, Tenika lights up as she speaks of her colleagues, her interactions, and her patient care there.

"I had Jewish OTs, I had Asian OTs, there were Black OTs, it was like the rainbow...it was. He [a co-worker] was having lunch one day and I asked what it was he was eating. I had never truly been around anybody who was Jewish because, being from the South, we were very sheltered; I didn't realize how much so until I got to New York. I asked what he was eating, and he said 'baklava.'"

Tenika says that her co-worker's wife made the baklava for her several weeks later and the experience of being introduced to this new food resulted in her learning about her co-worker...and much more. To her surprise, she gained insight and open mindedness. She noticed that "he [her co-worker] didn't feel judged when I asked him." This allowed her to conclude that "maybe if you start to soften some and start to allow people to be themselves, you can be more yourself—the more genuine version of you, and not this hard exterior. It definitely makes you more personable and more relatable with your clients, because your clients are a melting pot as well." Tenika's experience in New York was almost the opposite of what she had endured as a student. She called them family. She felt wanted. It was very different from the second part of her career, as she describes, that in the South it was "know your place, stay in your place."

When you are a new graduate of any profession, it is important to learn who you are as an individual first so that you can better equip yourself to take on the needs of others you may be in contact with throughout your day. Tenika confesses that she is very outspoken, has a type A personality, and does not need a microphone to communicate. She also understands that everyone does not do well with those personality traits. She explains:

> "It took a minute for me to gain that knowledge. You have to realize you have to temper what you say, because not everyone grew up the way that you did. Not everyone had the same rules and regulations. They didn't have the same parents in the same room; you have to take that into consideration. Even though you may have the same degree and you may have gone to the same school, you may even have the same nationality or whatever, your life experiences are not the same. So, they're going to mold the personality, they're going to mold the brain, they're going to mold the emotional foundation, that you have to deal with confrontation, or people who disagree."

Tenika has had a plethora of discriminatory interactions with co-workers and patients over the years. "I can give you pages of material on that." She has been called a housekeeper by a patient when attempting to start a treatment session and has even been told "I am not scared of you" when attempting to be autonomous in her OT treatment with her physical therapy co-worker. So many times, Tenika has been judged as many of us on the margins may have shared this experience. The layers of thick skin that were needed to survive are also the ones that need to be peeled back when trying to be client-centered in such a holistic profession as OT. For the sake of giving and assisting in healing others, we often lose sight of what makes that healing possible in the first place: the ability to present our true selves, unapologetically.

To present our true selves, we must discover who we are introspectively and be aware of society's perceptions of us. Being a person of color in the US is not a new adventure to be embarked on in the middle of one's life. This journey starts at birth. From new interactions to professional relationships and back to daily tasks like trips to the grocery store, it is not something that ever leaves you. When asked if this experience of her OT journey was a surprise, Tenika pauses briefly, and tearfully proceeds to say:

> "No, I will say no. In my opinion, Black females are the most under-rated, disrespected, and disregarded beings in the world. From music, social media, fashion, healthcare professions, just...no. I'm really getting emotional now because it's almost as if I expected it."

Tenika goes on to say:

> "I think a lot of that is from my mom from what she did – from integrating into high school, and what she had told me for years. I was just trying to deal with it. That's the thing you have to do. If you have to transfer in your fourth year of your last semester and start over, that's what you do and you keep going. So, I expected the disrespect. I was expected to be outcast. I expected it because I had it so often growing up."

As OT practitioners, adapting and modifying is what we do. We are the experts in task analysis and goal setting, and modifying those goals if we do not meet them. We need to remember that this skill does not stop at the transference to those we serve, but continues with us as well. As Tenika's path has progressed, she has found herself adapting and modifying her goals along the way, which has allowed her to grow into the best parts of herself through her experiences. This is something all health professionals (or occupational therapists) should do.

> "I would like that to be part of my legacy, so I'm going to reach back and try to help as many people as I can to attain the same success that I have. I'd love it if once I retire people remember me and say, 'Dr.

Danley really helped me. She was one of the professors who actually took time and fed into me, and helped me develop as a clinician.'"

REFLECTION QUESTIONS

1. Can you recall specific times in your life where your character and value were questioned? If so, what were the situations?
2. What do you hope your legacy is as you embark on this journey as a health professional?
3. What are some challenges you foresee for yourself? How can you best prepare yourself?
4. What "survival techniques" do you use as you move through your journey to become an occupational therapist? Are they specific to you?

Chapter 5

I Choose to Love

ALAA ABOU-ARAB

There are many words in the English language that are used both as a noun and a verb. For example, you can visit the park, or you can park your; you can read a book or book a flight. Love is probably the most popular of these terms. You can fall in love with someone or something and you can commit an act of love.

Joseph is a first-generation Ghanian (West Africa) American male, and he chooses to love every time. Black or African Americans make up approximately 5% of occupational therapists in the US. Black males make up an even smaller percentage. There are an estimated 1000 Black male OTs in the US—less than 1% of the total number of OTs in the US (American Occupational Therapy Association, 2020). Further portraying the power imbalance inherent in these statistics, it doesn't stop at the clinical level, or occupational therapy for that matter. Things aren't much better in higher education, across healthcare and other fields of study. In 2018, of the almost one million full-time faculty members at all degree-granting institutions, 69% of those were white, 5% were Black and Latino, and 10% were Asian American (Broady et.al., 2021).

Joseph was born and raised in the US, but his parents were both born in Ghana, so he says he is Ghanaian. That is where his culture stems from. His mother was a nurse and he knew he always wanted to be in healthcare.

"Nursing wasn't for me. I went through every health profession that exists and the one that sparked the lightbulb in me was occupational therapy. It gave me the capacity to do everything I was gifted to do. I believe I am not only helping people physically, but mentally and spiritually as well."

His undergraduate experience reveals similar characteristics to those portrayed in many of the chapters of this book, most of his classmates being white, and facing the challenges of navigating academia having come from a minoritized background. His OT school experience was quite different. Joseph went to Howard University, a historically Black college and university (HBCU).

"I went to one of the most popular HBCUs there is. It opened another door. I didn't know life could be like that. It felt like family, most of my professors were African American. I felt supported, it was very vibrant, I felt as if my voice was heard. I wouldn't have got through and been as successful as I am if I hadn't been to Howard University. They were behind me. I felt so much more comfortable with my journey into OT because I was in an HBCU. I wouldn't have taken as much initiative if I didn't attend an HBCU."

Within the justice, equity, diversity, and inclusion (JEDI) spaces, you'll hear a lot about how important *representation* is and its impact on the success of students of color. It's more than the things we hear about in the media. Every so often we are reminded of this representation when someone accomplishes something that hasn't been seen before from someone of a particular background or ethnicity. The "first Black head coach to win a Super Bowl" or the "first Asian American to win an Academy Award for best director"— these accomplishments are worth celebrating. But in Joseph's case, it was the everyday representation that an HBCU can provide that truly offered a sense of normalcy and calmness during what are often stressful times, navigating new adulthood and graduate school. The majority of occupational therapy students are white and go to predominantly white institutions, and with that comes the privilege of not having to navigate graduate school while simultaneously coping with racist systems.

There are 107 HBCUs in the US and they enroll close to 14% of all African American and Black students nationwide. HBCUs have led the way in generating African American students for health professions (Eubanks, 2019). With the US becoming more and more racially diverse, healthcare professions have long sounded the alarm to improve their racial demographics. Without HBCUs, this will not be attained. Eubanks says that the nurturing environment is advantageous to the success of these African American and Black students. Research suggests (as does this book) that students of color in OT programs fall victim to isolation and marginalization. Kitchens and colleagues conducted a study in 2022 exploring the experiences of Black and African American students in entry level OT and OTA programs. Participants in the study described barriers such as a lack of faculty and staff support, financial concerns, and a lack of comfort in sharing their life and cultural perspective (Kitchens *et al.*, 2022). Joseph's comfort level and the support he received during his OT school journey cannot be overstated. It had a direct impact on his success.

He began his OT career in a skilled nursing facility (SNF). "I started off in the nursing homes, waiting for my hand therapy job. I've always wanted to do hands. That's what first attracted me to OT." Occupation to Joseph means one word: "purpose." "Everyone thinks of it as a job or something you do. But to me, occupation is a source of happiness in life. The worst form of torture is doing nothing. We are all meant to do something in this world." Joseph's job as a hand therapist is to help patients after an injury or trauma to bridge the gap and get back to what they love to do. Culture and identity are important in Joseph's therapeutic approach. "Identity plays a large role in our occupations; it makes an impact. Identity is who you are, no two fingerprint are the same." As much as we love to provide a client-centered approach, we are interdependent on our environments and social systems.

"If there is a musical concert going on, someone must play the guitar, someone must play the drums, and at the same time, someone must be able to hold the camera to record the whole thing. Each of these people will identify themselves as an important puzzle piece. Your identity, your culture, your background really helps create that unified success that is needed."

Given that there aren't many Black male occupational therapy practitioners, one can empathize with the potential negative experiences Joseph must navigate daily. The common denominator for Joseph is that his patients often identify themselves not by race or gender, but as failures, looking at themselves and what they used to be able to do—a deficit-based way of thinking. He begins his treatment and evaluation sessions by choosing to love and empathize. "It all starts with the mind. I am big on people seeing the best of themselves and to see things through the lens of opportunity." Approaching differences in race, religion, or gender can be a delicate balance, but for Joseph his approach, again, is with love.

"Before I do anything with a patient, I ask them, 'How are you?' I can have my own bias and stereotypes. By asking them 'How are you?' it allows them to introduce their identity and the moment this is introduced, even if it is someone I don't know, it becomes more than the injury that I am treating, it becomes a place where I can see the human in them and provide the most client-centered intervention. I see so many different people every day – someone with a thick accent, or a certain religious background. I must be able to understand that every human who comes to me isn't the same, but we all have a purpose to fulfill in this world. We fulfill that purpose through our doing, our work, and our occupations."

Joseph's experiences aren't always positive, but he continues with the same approach. He has experienced discrimination from colleagues, finding out that he was being paid less than a non-Black co-worker doing a similar job. "It didn't make any sense." He has multiple minoritized identities and has had experiences no one should go through. "I try not to take things personally. My co-workers are cool, there is a colleague I probably wouldn't take to lunch. There are always those

people out there that aren't comfortable talking to a Black male."
Readers should take note of this description of discomfort. It is not
Joseph's responsibility to fix that discomfort, he didn't do anything to
cause that discomfort. All he is doing is being himself. For those who
hold these biases and witness this discomfort inside when speaking or
engaging with minoritized voices, do not put the onus on the minoritized person to ease your discomfort. That is your responsibility.

Experiences like these aren't isolated to our colleagues or mana-
gers. Minoritized OTs can be exposed to it from patients and clients
as well. "A patient walked into a session and blurted out, 'I don't want
to be treated by a Black therapist.' He was joking, but it was still
offensive." Joseph played it cool, as he always does, choosing to love
to conquer evil. But there is no excuse for that behavior.

> "I get patients all the time who start cold, but my threshold for pain
> has increased to where there is no one I can't treat. There are also
> moments with patients that are unforgettable in a positive way. I had
> this one Caucasian lady who was an advocate for Black history. She
> was all for African American culture, she even talked about how she
> pleaded with her family members about our causes. It opened my
> eyes even more. You can't judge a book by its cover."

Joseph's worldview and approach as an OT is founded on a firm belief
in loving thy neighbor. "I am a Christian, I don't fight evil with evil, I
choose love. I am a believer in that Jesus died for us and gave us the
way to eternal life." His favorite occupation is writing and sharing
poems that deliver this message. "Poetry allows us to see the beauty
God created in us. I think the Bible is very poetic. I love to dive in
deep, learning, and sharing that in a poetic way that is digestible
to folks." Joseph acknowledges that there is a big gap for African
Americans. "Things aren't great out there for African Americans."
Our personal experiences and our backgrounds are an essential
asset in implementing the therapeutic use of self, which is the use
of our personalities, our perceptions, and insights as a part of our
intervention and therapeutic process (Taylor *et al.*, 2009). Joseph's
biggest tool in his therapeutic toolkit is love. He understands that

these systems aren't meant for him to succeed, and he is fighting back and filling the gap the only way he knows how, with love.

REFLECTION QUESTIONS

1. This chapter shares the statistics of how Black OTs make up less than 1% of the US occupational therapy practitioner population. As much as Joseph demonstrates compassion through love, there is a greater issue of representation here. What are some ways as occupational therapy practitioners, can we increase representation in the OT field?
2. How does spirituality or religion guide your practice? How do you use it? If you don't use it, how do you approach a client or colleague who is spiritual or religious?

References

American Occupational Therapy Association (2020). *AOTA 2019 Workforce and Salary Survey*. Retrieved from: https://library.aota.org/AOTA-Workforce-Salary-Survey-2019.

Broady, K., Perry, A.M., & Romer, C. (2021). Underfunding HBCUs Leads to an Underrepresentation of Black Faculty. Brookings Institution. Retrieved from: www.brookings.edu/articles/underfunding-hbcus-leads-to-an-underrepresentation-of-black-faculty.

Eubanks, T.R. (2019). The Anatomy of it All: The Role of HBCUs in Producing Healthcare Professionals. *NACADA: Voices of the Global Community*, 42(3). Retrieved from: https://nacada.ksu.edu/Resources/Academic-Advising-Today/View-Articles/The-Anatomy-of-it-All-The-Role-of-HBCUs-in-Producing-Healthcare-Professionals.aspx.

Kitchens, R.F., Armstead, A.B., Mani, K., Ghulmi, L., & Collins, D.M. (2022). Exploring the experiences of Black/African American students in entry level occupational therapy and occupational therapy assistant programs: A survey study. *Journal of Occupational Therapy Education*, 6(2). Retrieved from: https://doi.org/10.26681/jote.2022.060202.

Taylor, R.R., Lee, S.W., Kielhofner, G., & Ketkar, M. (2009). Therapeutic use of self: A nationwide survey of practitioners' attitudes and experiences. *American Journal of Occupational Therapy*, March/April, 63(2), 198–207.

Chapter 6

I Have Always Been an OT

ALAA ABOU-ARAB

Before being able to practice occupational therapy in the US, you must be licensed in your respective state. To receive licensure, you will have to sit and pass the certification exam administered by the National Board for Certification in Occupational Therapy (NBCOT). To be eligible to take the exam, you must have earned a master's degree from an accredited OT program that typically takes two to three years to complete. The process is long and expensive. This book isn't just about that process of becoming an OT in the US. Our journeys do not start after admission to an OT program and they don't end after we finish our training. Our histories are both distinctive and diverse. An often-made mistake is painting minoritized individuals and groups with a wide brush. This book's objective is to share the differences within and among minoritized groups. These differences are illustrated throughout the lifespan. This text includes stories of some people who are descendants of refugees, or in fact refugees themselves. Although they might have fled from the same war, the histories and experiences are unique to each family. Kuma was a child refugee from Vietnam and arrived in Camden, New Jersey with his family after a long journey that started with fleeing from the war.

"I identify as a Cambodian American, but we were born in Vietnam, which can be confusing, but Vietnam has over 100 different ethnic groups. We are Khmer, one of the ethnic groups in the lower Mekong Delta. My family are from there. South Vietnam used to be part of Cambodia but because of French colonization, it became what is modern Vietnam. My parents escaped the Vietnam war, and we ended up in the US. To be exact, Camden, New Jersey is where I grew up, and if you know anything about Camden – do a quick Google search – you know, it's considered one of the top five most dangerous cities in the United States. Crime, poverty, you name it, we have it. I grew up in that environment and went to public school my whole life."

After graduating high school, Kuma wasn't sure what he wanted to do next. He wasn't certain if college was for him and he strongly considered joining the military. "I didn't think I was smart enough to go to college and the military was always at our high school." Ironically, the US military has been an all-volunteer service since the end of the Vietnam war in 1973 and has long been recruiting at high schools across the country, specifically in low-income areas (Camacho, 2022). This became even more apparent after then President George W. Bush signed the No Child Left Behind Act in 2002, which put schools at risk for losing federal funding if they did not provide the military recruiters the same personal information they provide to colleges and universities (Camacho, 2022). "My family dissuaded me; my dad was very upset that I wanted to join the military. After a long conversation, I decided to give college a shot." Kuma applied to a few schools and got into one. "I got in because of a program called the Equal Opportunity Fund (EOF)." The EOF in New Jersey provides supportive services (financial, counseling, tutoring) to students in the state who are from poor backgrounds.

"To be honest, I really wanted to be a graphic designer. Then, I don't know, I just felt unsatisfied and intimidated. My classmates were making amazing designs, coding, and all that stuff and I was nowhere near that. I went to public high school in Camden, and we didn't have computer science so I was playing a lot of catch up, so I decided to change majors."

Kuma always enjoyed working out, he was into fitness and shifted to exercise science, with the thought of working with athletes in the future. Before he was able to graduate, he had to complete an internship. He was guided to investigate areas of interest outside athletics, such as physical therapy and rehabilitation. He began his internship at a trauma hospital in Camden. Little did he know, he was going to shadow not only physical therapists in the hospital, but also speech and language pathologists, and, yes, occupational therapists. "I did my thing, and I followed all three disciplines, but I just felt like there was a connection to me and the OT. I started digging in deeper." Kuma started asking more questions and then finally asked his colleague how to get into OT school. The OTs at the hospital gave him the rundown. "They told me take the science courses, the GRE, and so on." Kuma felt as if he had found what he was looking for and applied to OT school. "I got into one of the four programs I applied to and I was scared out of my mind. I didn't think I was good enough for graduate school. But I knew in my heart that if I put all my effort into this, I would get through it."

His OT school experience began with a summer course and it started off well. "I met some great people that summer and we are friends to this day." The following semester, in the fall, as part of a service-learning project in OT school, Kuma was placed at a preschool in an area of the city decimated by poverty. Kuma loved working with the kids. "I could be silly; that comes naturally to me." It was an inclusive school that had children on the autism spectrum and with other developmental needs. Kuma's OT brain was already at work in that first full semester of OT school. He worked at a local aquarium while in high school and thought of getting the kids at the preschool, and their families, some tickets to visit the aquarium. "I thought that would be great for the families, as they had told me that they'd never been to the aquarium, not even a museum." Kuma reached out to his old colleague and asked for some tickets. "She didn't hesitate, she said, 'How many tickets do you need?'" Kuma, along with other students and staff, organized a day for these families to attend the aquarium. "It was amazing that I was able to make this happen. Everyone really enjoyed themselves. We got great feedback."

Although he was unsure of himself when he began OT school, this provided Kuma with validation of his decision to pursue OT. He started to see his career come into view. His mentor and colleague at the aquarium thought that this project could be the beginning of something more consistent. With guidance from a faculty advisor and in collaboration with the aquarium, they applied for grant to help create and sustain the project. As he was finishing his last year of OT school, the grant was awarded. By the time he graduated OT school, Kuma had already used many of the skills of an occupational therapy practitioner. His activism for access and inclusion is at the core of how we should practice. He had accomplished a lot, even before graduation, before he got into OT school. Kuma got his first OT position at the trauma hospital that he volunteered at before OT school. He had come full circle. They had hired him under a temporary license, and he began practicing while studying to take the exam. Now, all he had left to do was take and pass the NBCOT exam.

> "I had a direction in my mind: I will graduate OT school and go back to the hospital that I volunteered at. It was close to home, and I could continue to work on my aquarium project. But then I obviously had to take and pass the exam if I wanted to keep working there. So, I took my boards and I failed. I took it a second time, and I didn't pass. They had to let me go. My temporary license had lapsed, and the grant money clearly wasn't enough. I needed to work, and this led to a long struggle in my life to try and be an OT. I couldn't practice as an OT, because I couldn't pass the exam. After multiple, multiple attempts, I just couldn't pass. I studied so hard and, you know, did all these amazing things in the OT world, but I couldn't become an OT just because NBCOT said so. I had to work though, and I tried to find work that would allow me to use my OT skills. I always felt as if I was an occupational therapist."

Kuma continued working on his aquarium project and got a role as a job coach for a local community center. He felt some fulfillment in this role as he was able to use some of the skills that he developed in his OT training. Job coaches support individuals to perform in the workplace. OT practitioners are trained to assess the individual performance factors, as well as the social, cultural, political factors of the workplace, school, hospital, and so on. It was a good consolation for Kuma, but he wasn't satisfied. "I got to point in my life where I thought that maybe I needed a change of scenery." His significant other at the time suggested he think about traveling. "She told me I didn't have to stay in a job that I didn't like, and I could always find other ways to make a living, in other places, not just the US." He took a leap of faith, resigned from his position as job coach and took a break from life in the US. "We ended up going to Vietnam, back to the country where I was born."

Kuma and his significant other parted ways approximately nine months after they moved there, but he had connected with many people in the time he had spent there.

> "Funnily enough, I ended up meeting an OT from the Philippines. She was in Vietnam working for a company that offered services to kids in international schools. She asked me, 'What's your plan? Do you plan on staying in Vietnam for a while?'"

Kuma's new friend was inquiring about Kuma's future because she had resigned from the company and begun working for herself, freelancing. She was getting busier and busier, so she offered Kuma an opportunity. "She connected me with one client, just to see how it goes." Kuma began with one client but then his caseload began to grow. His friend who referred his first client ended up taking on another opportunity outside Vietnam and because he had made a name for himself and proved his wonderful skills as an OT, she referred her entire caseload to him. He was now a full-time OT practitioner in Vietnam.

> "I ended up staying in Vietnam and working as an OT full time. I had so many kids. I was covering four international schools: a Canadian international school, an American international school, a British inter-national school, and an Australian international school. So, I had kids

who had, you know, development delays and/or were on the autism spectrum. I was working with students inside the school and some in their homes. I was working with teachers, training parents and caregivers. The doors opened so wide in Vietnam. I presented to various international schools on how to help kids with autism. Most of the international schools didn't have OT or PT [physical therapy]. I even connected with a non-governmental organization in Hanoi and presented to a few hospitals there. I trained doctors and nurses in rural areas, along with community health workers. It was a cool experience and an amazing journey."

A few years went by and Kuma met his current partner. She was from South Africa and worked as an English teacher in Vietnam. They were traveling all over Southeast Asia, and Kuma was relishing in his OT experience. Then came the Covid-19 pandemic and everything changed. "Like everywhere else, things just kind of stopped. I went from having a full caseload to having two or three students." It was a big adjustment for Kuma and his partner. Professionally and financially, it was very difficult. They weren't sure if they wanted to stay in Vietnam. They decided to stick it out in Vietnam but then the pandemic continued beyond that first year. There were still many restrictions and Kuma was seeing some of his clients virtually, but it was getting harder and harder. "When it got into the second year of the pandemic, we weren't sure if we could sustain this life." Like a few years back in New Jersey, Kuma was looking elsewhere again. He knew he wanted to be an OT, wherever they decided to go. "I wanted to know where I could practice or how to continue practicing OT." They decided on Australia. Kuma researched the criteria to become licensed in Australia. They don't require passing the NBCOT exam, but the process is long and stringent, nonetheless. "I applied, shared all of my experience. I got approved, and now I am a full-time OT in Australia."

Kuma now works as a community/home-based OT, servicing clients from across the lifespan with physical dysfunction, autism spectrum disorders, mental health issues, and so on. His OT experience now involves assessments, interventions, and analysis of occupation that spans three continents. Kuma's robust experience has broadened his view of what occupation means. "It's how you live your life. It doesn't matter if you're 65 years old with mental health needs or a five-year-old with autism, it's our job to help you find a way to live your life." Our roles and values within cultural norms play a big part in Kuma's worldview and he's seen so much.

> "I am from Camden, with Black and Brown communities. Then I was in Philadelphia, more Black, Brown and Asian communities. Obviously Vietnamese people in Vietnam, and now I'm in Australia, where we have a lot of national and regional native people. There are of course white Australians and there are many other ethnic groups. I have had a lot of cultural exchanges."

There was an exchange in Australia that resonated with Kuma, bringing his career journey full circle once again.

He was given a telehealth consult, a teenager needing OT for a wheelchair evaluation. She was on a waiting list for OT and when Kuma saw her name, he said to himself, "That looks like a Cambodian name. I don't do this often, but I asked her if she was by any chance Cambodian." The client was in fact of Cambodian descent and from the same region of South Vietnam as Kuma. "We started talking and her mom came on the screen and was like 'oh my god' and we all started laughing and talking about things we shared." There was an instant connection and the similarities to his experience growing up as a Khmer American in Camden began to emerge. "They couldn't believe they had a Khmer OT." Like Kuma, the client comes from a poor background. It reminded him of his journey, his perseverance, and what it meant to this client to see the representation of Khmer people. "The entire time with this client was amazing and I haven't had that feeling with a client anywhere else, not in Philly, Camden, or Vietnam."

Some of Kuma's favorite occupations that initiated his transfer from graphic design to exercise science have also helped him through some perilous times. He still loves to be physically active, working out, playing soccer, and running. "I'd have to say Jiu Jitsu is my favorite occupation now. I have been doing this for a couple of years." Kuma does it every chance he gets. "It's my addiction now. It's an outlet for me and I still have ten years of training to become a black belt." He is now a husband and a father. He's always used an OT lens. He is an OT, he always was, and he always will be.

> "I left my own country to become an OT somewhere else. That's my journey. You might not pass your boards the first or second time. If you want to be an OT, don't give up."

REFLECTION QUESTIONS

1. How do you measure failure? Is it dependent on your expectations? Your parents? Someone else (your professor, mentor)?
2. How much emphasis do you place on culture when measuring what is a success and what is a failure?
3. How do you cope with failure? How does it impact what's important to you?

References

Camacho, R. (2022). Military recruiters are increasingly targeting Latinx students for enlistment. Sept. 19, 2022. *Prism*. Retrieved from: prismreports. org.

Chapter 7

Kiddush Hashem

ERICA V. HERRERA

To be any kind of human in this world comes with a long list of labels, characteristics, and associations. As time has passed, humans have not stopped taking opportunities to represent their cultures, religions or even their race, respective to the regions of the world in which they reside. For Libby, her identity is wrapped in a coil of race, religion, region, and global catastrophe. It is possible that if we individually took the time to research our histories back far enough, we could find our identities described in the same manner. For Libby, the links to her foundation are recent in the timeline of history.

Libby's grandparents were both born in Romania. They were both at Auschwitz, in the Holocaust. Although her grandparents didn't know each other at the time they were taken from their homes in Romania, they were actually distant cousins. "They were the only ones, aside from one sibling each, from their family who survived the Holocaust, out of eight or nine siblings. They found each other when they were back in Romania and got married." Libby's parents were born in Romania, then moved to Israel. Some may look at Libby's history with sorrow or awe or maybe even admiration. What does hold true, is the survivorship that occurred among Jewish people all over the world, and how that history is reflected in the lives of their descendants. The events that took place during and surrounding the Holocaust continued to affect and spread into families as well as other Jewish people (Lazar & Litvak-Hirsch, 2009). Unless you are directly connected to this group of people, as Libby is, it can be hard to fathom that a few generations ago, there was the threat of complete annihilation of Jewish people. It is history like this that shapes our identities, whether we are aware of it or not.

Libby's grandparents had family in Chicago and eventually started their own family there, which included Libby's mother and aunts. Libby's mother would soon return to Israel where she met Libby's father and later had Libby. As a baby, Libby was brought to the US by her mother, and she grew up in Chicago. Libby explains, "We go to Israel all the time to visit my in-laws because my husband is also from there. I feel that even though I'm an Israeli, I'm an American too, you know? I have dual citizenship, but I grew up mostly here in the States." To be a part of two places can be a blessing and a burden at the same time. Trying to stay true to religious and moral beliefs from one area, while connecting and abiding by the greater community where you reside in another area, can definitely be challenging. Libby depicts this more by expressing:

"It's the holidays there...everything closes, and on Saturday with the Sabbath. It is just so different there. You don't feel like you have to work so hard to maintain your identity, or your Judaism in Israel. It is very hard [to maintain your identity] when you grow up here in the States, but I already have a home and a life here."

Libby goes on to say that although America, and many of its comforts, is home, Israel holds aspects of her spirituality. She says:

"It's tricky. I guess I have mixed emotions. I grew up here. I came here when I was three months old, so this is all I know. Now, every time I go to Israel, I feel as if I probably should stay. Then I come back to the States and I'm like, 'Oh, thank god I'm home.'"

Libby's internal conflict may be one that many of us have experienced because of the complexities of human identity. As Libby reflects on the different aspects of herself, so do many others around the world. Not only do we question and define our identities, daily, but we also project them in all that we do, consciously and unconsciously, at work, school, home and even on a greater scale, in politics and healthcare.

"I've always been very artistic, so when I was in college I majored in art. I thought I was going to be an art therapist. I started volunteering here and there in a hospital. While at the hospital, we were doing some little things and all of a sudden next door I heard all these kids jumping, and people were making a noise. I went over there and everyone was playing with balls and on swings. I said, 'What is this?' They said, 'This is occupational therapy.' I was thinking, 'Wow, this is really cool. I want to learn.' It is cool how it happened because I love science, but I didn't want to be a doctor, that's too much. I love to be creative, and you need to be like an artist, so it was the best of both worlds. [Occupational therapy] just clicked."

When it comes to the actual name of our profession, Libby has never been very fond of it.

"I don't think I'm the only one, I think there are other people also. The name just really doesn't define the profession. I wouldn't even know what to name it but when you introduce someone to an occupational therapist and they don't know what it is they're like, 'Well, what are you going to do with my occupation?'"

With all of the confusion that may come with the term, there is a lot of beauty in its vagueness as well. Libby captures this when she says:

"Occupational therapy looks at the person's whole self, not just their medical condition. That's what I love about it because it considers what is going on in your daily living that may affect treatment out-comes. I look at my 'whole' self as well, factoring in the balance of trying to be a good therapist and caring for my family, without overloading myself."

Libby's definition is beautiful because as occupational therapy practitioners we serve deeply and willingly while attempting to maintain the fullness in our own cups. This is a lesson in task analysis itself.

Not everyone who enters occupational therapy school does so directly from a college or university. They may also have other life circumstances which require them to juggle and sacrifice certain priorities. In Libby's case, she started to get her bachelor's degree in New York, but then she met her now husband when she was young. She came back to Chicago and completed a fast-track bachelor's in arts and Judaic studies. By then, she already had got married and had her first baby. "I remember dancing in the kitchen with my newborn when I got my acceptance letter." Libby jokingly continues, "School was so time consuming that I didn't get a lot of time to spend with my son. When I graduated, two days before my second child's birth, I'm like, 'Whoa, you're two years old already! Look at you!'" Family dynamics are challenging, especially when embarking on a professional career. We never know what our colleague, classmate, or student may be experiencing but it is safe to say that support of any kind is greatly appreciated.

Libby recalls how her time in OT school was challenging because there wasn't anyone else who identified with her religion and its customs the way that she did. She says, "It was really hard because there wasn't anyone else. Being Jewish and being orthodox are two different things. There are different levels of religion." Like other monotheistic religions, there are differences within Judaism. In the US, there are approximately six million individuals who identify as Jewish (about 2.5% of the adult population). Close to only 10% of American Jews identify as orthodox (Pew Research Center, 2020). This is not to classify one type of practice above another, but for Libby, being orthodox means to follow the commandments that are outlined.

"Being orthodox, I keep Sabbath and all the Jewish holidays. School started in September, just as the Jewish holidays started, and I did not know any classmates. All of a sudden, I had to say, 'I need to take off for the Jewish holidays. Can you please help me with the notes?' There are more familiar holidays like Yom Kippur, the Day of Atonement and Rosh Hashanah, and the Jewish New Year. But there are other holidays that are lesser known."

Although Libby lived in a state that is considered to have one of the highest populations of Jewish people, Libby still felt "really isolated and really alone." It was not easy to carry out her customs while in school. Even within our own communities, made up of many people who may seem to have the same ideals, we can still have unique needs, where we require true support to reach our full potential.

Although grateful to be a part of a cohort of 60 students and thankful that she was able to complete her program, Libby's idea of what a supportive OT school should be (diverse, open-minded, and safe) didn't materialize. When it was time for her to participate in her Jewish holidays, her peers did not welcome her request for things like class notes, since they felt she was "playing hooky," as Libby puts it.

"They weren't orthodox, so it was so hard for them to understand the idea that Jewish holidays are like the Sabbath, with the same restrictions. I took this as an opportunity to educate others on the beauty of Judaism. I felt that it was beneficial for everyone in the long run because being exposed to different religions, as I was, makes one a more culturally diverse person. It helps a person grow as an occupational therapist but more importantly as a sensitive human being."

As an occupational therapy practitioner, Libby always thought she would work with kids but states:

"As my kids and their needs grew, that population did not seem to fit. I tried working after graduation but after having three young children it was getting more difficult. I was a latchkey kid myself because both my parents had to work full time, so I took advantage of the fact that I was fortunate enough to be able to be a stay-at-home mom."

Libby made the decision to take time off work in order to raise her growing family. It was ten years before she went back to OT practice, after having four children. She frustratingly recalls, "I did all of my continuing education units and paid for my license renewal. I actually got audited because I did everything on webinars and not at in-person seminars, but I had no choice. They accepted my credentials after I explained my situation." It is a blessing that the profession of OT allows us to maintain our status and licensure/registration as long as we keep up with our required courses and provide proof. However, to be a skilled practitioner also means we need to feel confident and comfortable in our area of practice. After trying to get back into OT after ten years, Libby shares, "I have to say it was scary going back to work after being away for so long and I was worried that my skills had waned. However, it was like riding a bike and it all came back to me quickly." Even though we may be tough on ourselves to provide the best care to our patients, it is surprising how much occupational therapy becomes a part of you in a way that you can perform, even after being gone for a while.

Libby's area of expertise is the geriatric population.

"I never thought I would work with the elderly, because growing up, my entire family owned and worked in geriatric facilities. I decided to give it a try and I absolutely love working with the elderly. I joke that I have so many sets of grandparents because I can associate with them so easily like family."

Although she has had wonderful experiences and continues to work in this area of practice, she has still felt that she stood out among the rest. "The patients learn about my religion and are very curious because more often than not I am the first orthodox Jew that they have encountered." Although at times, Libby may not feel confident in her OT skills after being gone for a period of time, she has always been confident in how she carried herself as an orthodox Jewish woman. She has welcomed the opportunity to educate others who are interested. Libby explains this more by saying, "It's a very big thing in our culture to represent it. If you're a good person and you act that way and people find out that you're an orthodox

Jew and you're the only one that they see, it is a huge responsibility, but in a good way." Libby is suddenly reminded of the Jewish term that encompasses what she is describing and that is Kiddush Hashem.

> "It's as if you're representing God the way you act. This is our belief, that we are created in the image of God. When you act properly and within your religious beliefs, that's how people think Jewish people should be. You represent the entire culture. I was the only one in the center where I worked and the only one in my OT school who was really orthodox, so it was important for me to represent the culture properly."

When you're working as an occupational therapist, there are many flexibilities in practice settings and schedules. Luckily, we can work full time, part time or per diem. Being an orthodox Jewish woman, Libby had to make sure to set her boundaries wherever she worked. She explains, "I can't work on Saturdays because of the Sabbath, and I have to leave earlier on Fridays in the winter when the sun sets earlier because that is when the Sabbath begins."

Although this seems like a lot of accommodation, it is her right and she is grateful for it.

> "I'm very lucky. I've been thinking about my grandparents and how they suffered during the Holocaust just because of their religion. Then after that, while in Romania, the country was not accepting of Orthodox Judaism, and my grandfather got fired from so many jobs because he wouldn't work on Saturday; but he wouldn't give up his belief. I learned so much from their sacrifices and want to continue their legacy by educating others and setting examples for my own family to follow."

Occupational therapy practitioners are trained in the therapeutic use of self. In short, this can be seen as a form of sharing. We don't just share information and techniques with our patient population, we also share parts of who we are, with those with whom we work.

Libby felt the most at peace when she was among her colleagues at the subacute care center she worked at. She explains, "We felt like a family there because we were there for eight years together. Everybody knew each other by name. Skin color didn't matter, religion didn't matter, we were all just one big family, which was so nice." This level of comfort aided in her ability to help her patients as well.

> "When people were bed-bound, it made me so sad. There was one obese woman who everybody had given up on. I made it part of her treatment plan to get her into a motorized wheelchair, which was her ultimate goal. Along with other disciplines, which I feel were key to helping her reach her therapy aims, her goal was accomplished. Working as a team is essential and I was so fortunate to be a part of such a great one so others could be therapeutically healed and regain their functional independence and their lives."

Maybe this is the best way to feel that we are "like everyone else." We allow our identities to represent us to the outside world and use that to advocate for our patients, our colleagues, and ourselves. Kiddush Hashem.

REFLECTION QUESTIONS

1. With our flexibility as occupational therapy practitioners, do you feel our current continuing education requirements are enough to keep us up to date and safely perform our patient care duties?
2. What do you think Libby means when she says she was "the only one"? Can you identify with this in any parts (past or present) of your life?
3. What does it mean to feel like everybody else? Is this innate, a societal influence, or both?

References

Lazar, A. & Litvak-Hirsch, T. (2009). Cultural trauma as a potential symbolic boundary. *International Journal of Politics, Culture, and Society*, 22(2), 183–190.

Pew Research Center (2020). Jewish Americans in 2020. Retrieved from: www.pewresearch.org/religion/2021/05/11/the-size-of-the-u-s-jewish-population.

Chapter 8

More Than the Model Minority

ALAA ABOU-ARAB

Sarah always felt lucky to have been born and raised in Southern California. With nearly 15% of the total population in Los Angeles County of Asian descent, it is the largest Asian population of any county in the United States (U.S. Census Bureau, 2021). Sarah is an only child to two Chinese-Vietnamese immigrants, who found their home in Southern California after fleeing Vietnam due to the war. "I identify more with my Chinese roots. We speak Cantonese and Teochew at home and celebrate Chinese holidays and traditions." Sarah's parents' journey involved fear and struggle. Their lives were completely overturned by the war. Many of Sarah's family members had their homes and possessions taken, and were even placed in jail or prison camps. It took them many attempts before they were able to escape. Originally sponsored by a church, her parents made their way from Vietnam to North Carolina and then eventually to California. Despite the trials and tribulations that her parents endured, she is grateful for the safety and security provided in her upbringing. "Living in 'SoCal' my whole life, I really grew up in a bubble, I wasn't a minority in my hometown."

That bubble expanded throughout her schooling and even as she entered the university setting. Many of the same individuals she knew in high school were attending the same university. "I already had my roommate picked out...even in college most of my friends were Asian." During her sophomore year in college, while at lunch with a friend, she was introduced to occupational therapy. Not having a formal plan for post-graduation, Sarah agreed to start volunteering. She did so at a pediatric clinic, a skilled nursing facility, and a local hospital. "I always enjoyed meeting new people and connecting with them and knew that was a strength of mine." She graduated with her undergraduate degree in business accounting, a major her mom had suggested for its job security, but which had never excited her. Her volunteer experiences made it apparent that OT was a better fit for her than accounting.

Not unlike other first-generation immigrant OT practitioners highlighted in this book, she felt pressure to succeed. That pressure wasn't just from her parents, but from herself as well. "I felt indebted to my parents, and I would've done anything to make them proud. I wanted to show them that their sacrifice was worth it." Growing up, Sarah's parents put her in extracurricular activities, including swimming, piano, art, Chinese school, and college prep courses. "My parents wanted to give me every opportunity they never had." Wanting a change of scenery, Sarah almost attended a university in Chicago for her OT training but ultimately decided to stay in Southern California for OT school. Sarah not only had to carry the weight of a first-generation immigrant, but also that of an only child. "My mom said if I went across the country, she would be very upset. Out of duty and also guilt, I decided to choose a school close to home."

The bubble she grew up in then continued into her OT training. "The majority of my classmates were Asian. I felt safe and understood among my peers. I never felt any judgment or disadvantage for being Asian." This experience highlights the necessity for representation of minoritized individuals in OT programs and workplaces. You'll see stark differences between those featured in this book, whose identities were represented well, and those who were the only ones or one of a few. Sarah was safe, she navigated OT school with minimal barriers as it related to her identity. "I didn't feel as if the stereotypes I experienced were necessarily negative at the time." She did well, graduated, passed her certification exam, and began her OT career.

Sarah's "bubble" and the belief that the stereotypes placed on her were not "negative" came from the socially constructed concept of the "model minority." This concept is harmful on many levels. First, it assumes that people of Asian descent are a monolith. This places the many diverse ethnicities, experiences, languages, and meaningful occupations into a very narrow lens. Occupational therapy practitioners are trained to look at the whole person when providing care, whereas this narrow view of the diversity within the Asian population leads to bias and discrimination. Second, this myth about Asian Americans and their perceived collective success has been used to minimize the role racism plays in the struggles of other minority groups, such as Black Americans. By using the label "model minority," it implicitly assumes that other minoritized individuals are a "problem" minority (Jagpal & Schumacher, 2022).

Then came 2020 and the Covid-19 pandemic. Anti-Asian sentiments led to an alarming increase in hate crimes and xenophobia directed toward Asian-Americans, and specifically Chinese Americans during the pandemic, which was first reported in China (Gover *et al.*, 2020). For Sarah, this was when she felt her "bubble" bursting. "I felt angry, scared, and really sad." The racism against those of Asian descent in the US is not new and is present throughout its history. People of Asian descent were stigmatized and excluded, particularly in America's Western states where they had immigrated as part of the Gold Rush. Anti-Asian sentiments were present in the late 1800s and early 1900s. For example, the Chinese Exclusion Act of May 6, 1882 suspended Chinese immigration and rendered Chinese immigrants ineligible for naturalization. Exclusion acts were repealed in 1943, but newer immigration policies significantly limited the number of foreign-born Chinese immigrants able to seek naturalization up to 1965 (Abou-Arab & Ashcraft, 2021).

The events in 2020 led Sarah to a personal realization. "Even though I knew the history of racism against Asian Americans, I was shielded from it my entire life. I had always been proud of my Chinese roots and the Asian stereotype had never negatively affected me… until it happened to me. I think I just really didn't know." Sarah and her family took a trip to Santa Barbara in California to celebrate her parents' anniversary. "It was meant to be relaxing, but it was during the height of all these anti-Asian hate crimes; we were all on edge and my dad even carried a stick with him, in case someone attacked us." A Pew Research study showed 32% of Asian American adults said they feared someone might threaten or physically attack them (Ruiz *et al.*, 2021). Another time in 2020, Sarah was walking in the city with her boyfriend Tim, who is also of Asian descent. A man approached them and shouted at Tim, "What are you looking at, motherfucker?" and threw a punch at Tim.

> "I don't know if he was ever going to hit him, Tim backed away, thank God, but he got so close to hitting him. I had never experienced something like that, so it just really scared me, even more so because of everything I was seeing on the news. I remember crying for a long time after that. That encounter stole my sense of security. It opened my eyes to what it's like to be targeted because of your race. It made me see a lot clearer. It gave me a glimpse of what people who are Black or Middle Eastern have dealt with."

Whether it was before or after the onset of the Covid-19 pandemic, identity played a significant role in Sarah's clinical approach. Identities involve meaningful things such as language and culture. She talks about how scary it might feel for someone who doesn't speak English. The fear of non-English-speaking patients and clients was real and personal for Sarah. "My grandma, who doesn't speak English, was hospitalized a few years ago. I saw first-hand how scary it is for those patients. My family and I took turns staying at the hospital so she was never alone, but they didn't allow us to go down with her for an MRI." The doctors told her family they weren't able to complete the MRI, stating that her grandmother was confused. They suggested giving her grandmother Ativan (a tranquilizer used to make individuals with anxiety feel calm) and try the MRI again.

> "I was appalled because my grandma is not confused. After talking with her, I learned that she was just scared because no one had taken the time to explain the procedure to her in a language she

understood. I always use an interpreter because I want my patients to feel safe in my care. I treat my patients how I wish my grandma was treated. I often see our non-English-speaking patients fall through the cracks, and that is not okay."

Sarah doesn't just identify as someone from Asian descent; she is also a woman and must carry these multiple marginalized identities into the workplace. Her identity as an Asian American in the workplace hasn't brought, in her words "discrimination," but as a woman she has felt it.

"People sometimes make inappropriate comments or touch me in ways that make me uncomfortable. I know many women in the workforce deal with this and it makes me so angry. Even though I know it's wrong, speaking up is scary because of the backlash or drama it might cause. When I feel empowered enough to say something, I've been met with comments like 'Why can you take a compliment?' or 'Why are you so sensitive?' I've got better at speaking up for myself, but it's upsetting that I need to."

Over 85% of the licensed OT practitioners in the US are women,[1] and these individuals must walk and breathe in these environments daily. Sarah's experiences are not isolated. These moments are what help us feel our identity. They influence the way we see our patients, our colleagues, and our peers. It's one of the things that makes Sarah an amazing OT. Sarah explains how she sees occupation: "I think it's anything someone wants or needs to be able to do in order to live a meaningful and happy life." As a hospital-based, acute care occupational therapist, this can be tricky.

"Working in a hospital, we don't have as many resources. Our patients are very sick and hooked up to lines and tubes. Our treatments can become very ADL [activities of daily living] focused, which I've

---

[1]   https://datausa.io/profile/soc/occupational-therapists

worked hard to break out of. I luckily work alongside creative and passionate OTs that inspire me."

As her experiences increase and she studies how other colleagues have occupation-based interventions within the acute care setting, Sarah's approach has changed.

"Instead of me being like, 'Hey this is what we're doing today,' I'll ask them, 'What do you want to do?' I like giving them that power; it makes them feel better about themselves... I'll never force someone to just walk with me to the bathroom."

She shares the story of a patient, a young woman who was a pediatric nurse. The woman was in the hospital for a severe nerve degenerating disorder that left her nearly blind. The patient was the mother of two young kids and a newborn baby. "I felt a connection with her. She was close to my age, a healthcare worker, and always so kind and gracious." The patient and the family progressed well with modifications presented to them. She mastered most basic ADLs quickly (i.e. dressing, bathing, toileting). Sarah felt as if there was more for her to do, despite it being in the acute setting. Often in the acute setting, meeting all of the long-term goals and performing basic ADLs at a standby assist level necessitates a discharge from OT services. You don't normally see patients doing higher level occupations, such as driving, cooking, or cleaning in the hospital setting. On her last session with this patient, Sarah walked into the patient's room with a baby doll (often used in the pediatric setting). She wrapped up the baby doll with weights to match the newborn's weight.

"We both started laughing when I walked into the room, but this is meaningful: She still wasn't able to do everything she was doing before. I had her walk around the room doing different activities while holding the baby and even change the baby's diaper. This activity was realistically what the patient would need to do once she returned home. It challenged her endurance and balance in a way that working on ADLs wouldn't – that's what matters."

If only every patient had Sarah for an OT. She shares a story of another patient, a young woman, a 19-year-old college cheerleader who had been admitted to the hospital for an autoimmune disease called neuromyelitis optica that affected her central nervous system. The patient experienced full body pain, seizures, blurry vision, and profound weakness in her lower extremities. "She stayed at our hospital for a month, and I was lucky enough to be her OT throughout her stay. She worked so hard despite her pain and medical setbacks. Her strength and resilience amazed me." Over the weeks, Sarah developed a strong bond with the patient on common interests such as a closeness with family, a love of cookies, and music. "She loved Jack Harlow, so I would play his songs during our sessions." OT practitioners working in acute care see many individuals every day. People are admitted to the hospital for a myriad of reasons, and often OT practitioners play an integral role in the recovery process and eventually in the discharge from the hospital to the next level of care. Whether that is at home or another facility to continue the recovery process, the OT probably won't ever see or hear from that patient again. Sarah's patient made tremendous gains, qualifying her to go to an acute rehabilitation unit (ARU) for more intensive rehabilitation. A few weeks after being discharged from the hospital, Sarah got an unexpected email from the patient's mother.

> "She told me that the patient was almost caring for herself independently now. She was climbing a flight of stairs and was finally discharged home from the ARU. Her mom said that the patient didn't remember much from her stay in the hospital but that I made a big impression on her and that the patient often asked about me. It is difficult to express how happy I was reading her email and how grateful I was to hear about the patient's recovery. Her email reminded me how much of an impact we make on our patients. Experiences like this make my toughest days a little easier and make me so thankful to be a part of such an awesome profession."

Sarah's empathy, compassion, and perspective resulting from her personal experiences led to an outstanding therapeutic moment that provided a validation not often received. Healthcare workers have to be at their best, especially when clients and patients are at their worst and most vulnerable. Sarah carries the weight as a direct descendant of refugees. She is a woman, an Asian American, and an occupational therapist, and for that she is much more than your model minority.

REFLECTION QUESTIONS

1. We often can't control how others who don't know us perceive us. Do the stereotypes of your ethnic or racial background impact how you identify? Do they impact the way you see your peers from similar backgrounds?
2. Was there a particular experience in your life, or the life of a loved one, that changed the way you look at identity?
3. How have these experiences impacted your ability to engage in meaningful activities or helped/hindered your clients to engage with you?

References

Abou-Arab, A. & Ashcraft, R. (2021). Trauma-Informed Care: Historical and Modern Implications of Racism and the Engagement in Meaningful Activities. In A. Lynch, R. Ashcraft, & L. Tekell (eds), *Trauma, Occupation, and Participation: Foundations and Population Considerations in Occupational Therapy* (pp.245–274). Bethesda, MD: AOTA Press.

Gover, A.R., Harper, S.B., & Langton, L. (2020). Anti-Asian hate crime during the COVID-19 pandemic: Exploring the reproduction of inequality. *American Journal of Criminal Justice*, 45(4), 647–667. Retrieved from: www.ncbi.nlm.nih.gov/pmc/articles/PMC7364747.

Jagpal, N., & Schumacher, M. (2022). Problem Minority & Model Minority: "Solidarity" Against the Backdrop of Anti-Blackness. Equity in the Center. Retrieved from: https://equityinthecenter.org/solidarity-backdrop-of-anti-blackness.

Ruiz, N., Edwards, K., & Lopez, M.H. (2021). One-third of Asian Americans fear threats, physical attacks and most say violence against them is rising. Pew Research Center. Retrieved from: www.pewresearch.org/ short-reads/2021/04/21/one-third-of-asian-americans-fear-threats-physical-attacks-and-most-say-violence-against-them-is-rising.

U.S. Census Bureau. (2021). About the topic of race. Retrieved from: www. census.gov/topics/population/race/about.htm.

Chapter 9

Mental Resilience

ERICA V. HERRERA

The Covid-19 pandemic has taught the world that the biggest potential threats to humanity do not have to be visible at all. Witnessing what viruses can do as well as the mental turmoil and social ineptitude experienced by many after the quarantine period, one could argue that we have experienced the worst internal war in history. Gritzer and Arluke (1985) educate us about the building blocks of occupational therapy profession in their book *The Making of Rehabilitation*. They found that the origins of occupational therapy could be traced back to ancient Egypt, where there was a noticeable relationship between activity and recovery from sickness. Furthermore, at the start of the 21st century, occupation or "work" was not only viewed as a remedy for physical ailments but mental illnesses as well. Striving for good mental health and wellness was one of the original aims of occupational therapy. Praveen gravitated toward this aspect of OT practice right from the start of his journey as a clinician.

Praveen is originally from India and then moved to Canada when he was eight years old. All of Praveen's family migrated to Canada and he spent a large part of his life in school there, until the age of 25. After college, he then went to the US to eventually pursue OT school. About 75% of Praveen's family is from the medical world and it was actually his mother who advised him, initially, to look into occupational therapy. His dad worked in dietetics, his mother was a nurse, and the extended family include doctors, physical therapists, nurses, and dentists. When Praveen witnessed occupational therapy in Canada, he was intrigued. Interestingly, Praveen and his younger siblings were much more on the creative side rather than the medical one—his brother is a musician and producer and his sister home-schools her son and has a background in management. Prior to going to OT school, Praveen was doing interior design and architectural drafting, which again are very creative spaces. Unbeknownst to him, he would be utilizing those creative spaces later in his OT career for the benefit of adolescents and students.

It is fascinating how we end up on our paths, considering where we start in life. Praveen's mother may have introduced the idea of OT to him in his younger years but it wasn't until later that it became something he truly considered. When Praveen moved to California, his girlfriend at the time was a physical therapist. She asked Praveen if he would consider physical therapy (PT), and he said he would. Praveen was accepted for PT school but went back and forth about whether this was truly the career choice for him. He observed PT in order to finish his required hours prior to the program but then realized that he did not want to go into that field after all. When Praveen told his counselor that he had declined his place on the program, she was in disbelief. The counselor explained to Praveen how hard it was to get onto a program and, as Praveen puts it, "she was freaking out." But Praveen felt that the career path just didn't suit him. It may have seemed a rash change of heart, but with hindsight, he made a great personal decision, just in time. Praveen and his counselor went back to the drawing board. She started to ask him questions such as, "Who are you?" "What are you like?" "What are your hobbies and your interests?" After Praveen shared some of his interests with her, such as his affinity to music and talking to people, she suggested he should be an OT practitioner. Praveen did not waste any time. He fine-tuned some of the prerequisite skills, completed his hours, and then got accepted into OT school.

As a faculty member now, Praveen often compares what he sees in programs today with when he was in OT school. There were roughly 30 students in his cohort. Praveen was in school around 1996 or 1997 and felt as though students were slightly older, with partners and families, than they are today. He also observes that many of the students are coming directly from college into the OT program and believes their worldviews and life lessons are still developing. For Praveen and many of his classmates, OT was their second career and they already learned how to be autonomous and work independently. In contrast, Praveen's experience as an educator has taught him that students are still working on being autonomous in a university setting. He understands that the students today are definitely smart but there are certain "street smarts" that are still developing. Praveen sees how the academic culture has shifted from learning the skills needed to be work ready, to a focus on maintaining a high grade point average (GPA). As time goes on, there will continuously be changes in all cultures, including academic culture. Therefore, it is important for the growth of our profession to understand the culture and identity of our students so that we can obtain the best outcome for their future.

Praveen noticed his class was mostly Caucasian but that did not bother him, nor was it his focus. As he looks back on the demographics of his class, he recalls a Filipino student, a Chinese student, two East Indian students, including himself, and one African American female student. Praveen remembers a particular incident—that seems to have been a microaggression—in OT school. He explains that the African American female student wasn't doing too well. Praveen, being Indian, was stereotyped by his faculty as someone who would get good grades, so they asked him to help her. It is a very interesting stereotype regarding intelligence and getting good grades. Praveen has noted this in his own Indian heritage but it is also said to be true about the neighboring region of East Asia. In their article "Prescriptive stereotypes and workplace consequences for East Asians in North America," Berdhal and Min (2012) found that in North America, there is a historical stereotype that East Asians are highly competent. This sounds like a compliment, doesn't it? But whether it is deemed positive or negative, assigning an assumption to an entire group is a form of racial bias. This is another example of the *model minority* concept, highlighted in Chapter 8.

Although Praveen worked hard in school, he acknowledges that he was a B student and felt that he was the wrong person to help his classmate. As well as being associated with a characteristic because of his race, Praveen also recalls a similar moment; however, this time it was because of his gender. Ironically, when he was starting OT school, Praveen did feel supported but for very different reasons. He explains, "Faculty supported me and kind of supported my representation. I don't think it was because I was East Indian but more so because I was a male. Interestingly, I think [being a male among mostly females] was what helped me." Often, there are so many aspects that someone may gravitate toward when they look at another individual. Is it their race, culture, or gender? What is important, first, is the individual and what that individual's focus is. For Praveen, he walked into the program with the objective to become an occupational therapist. The rest is history.

As a clinician, Praveen has mostly been in a mental health setting. He states, "I wanted to do mental health, right from the beginning. There's something inside me that is mental health, but I did not know that until I started my field work." Praveen does not feel that he gained much knowledge from his mental health course in school. The spark came when he saw what unfolded during his field work. He enjoyed the group process of therapy and didn't realize he would end up working as a pediatric mental health specialist, in an inpatient setting. "I thought I was going to do adult mental health, but no. Turns out [mental health with] adolescents aged 14–17 is what I love to do." Many times, we go into school thinking we are bound to one practice area. However, we grow and we learn what might suit us best for a particular season in time. For Praveen, that season has lasted over 20 years. Praveen expands on this by explaining how he has always been a deep thinker. "I've always been that person who looks at things from different angles and has conversations about it." When we are providing skilled care as occupational therapists, we cannot disconnect the person from the clinician; we are living in the same body. The result of that is a collection of controlled thoughts, ideas, and emotions which span time and are brought into the sessions we lead. It is no different for Praveen.

"The eight-year-old is in there, the 16-year-old is in there, the 18-year-old is in there. I can relate to these kids, because that eight-year-old experienced bullying or that 16-year-old experienced a really bad breakup or there was conflict with parents. I've seen that child in me, he's still there...[and that is] when I can connect with them."

As an occupational being, Praveen reminds us again of his love for music and all aspects of it. Playing, writing, and listening to music provides him with a deep joy. He also enjoys photography and even the task of looking at great photos, not just taking them. So, what is "occupation" to a mental health specialist?

"Occupation, to me, is part of human nature, where we are constantly, twenty-four-seven engaged with some activity, some tasks. Whether it is sleeping, eating, socializing, or relaxing, occupation is a constant movement. In my life, it's fluid. And if there's a place where it gets impaired, I have to figure out how to reset or work around that because it addresses my well-being. Occupation is also mental health, so in other words, exercising our ability to mentally be resilient and still engage."

Sometimes it can be difficult to engage in your occupation because of outside factors. Praveen worked for a home health agency for a short time in his career. He would go into certain houses, have certain experiences, where he just felt the tension in the air. In home health, you generally get approximately six visits approved by a health insurance company. There were times when the patient would quickly say to Praveen, 'Oh I don't need you anymore, you don't need to come.' Praveen even recalls a time where he and a PT colleague, who was also East Indian, had to take a call at the same time to a home health site. Praveen shares, "He walked out and he said, 'Did you feel that?' I said, 'Oh yeah, hundred percent.' So, we called the agency and said we didn't want to go there again." Although Praveen was alerted by these situations, he was not thrown off by them. He says it was a part of his upbringing and that he was subjected to racism even before becoming an adult.

"I don't want to say I'm numb to it, but what I've done is I've laid on a thick coat to pick my battles. Some battles are pointless. Yes, some battles I'm going to have to say, 'Do you understand what you're saying to me?' I might have to confront them. Part of my upbringing was understanding values and morals and knowing who I am. If I know who I am, what they think of me is no big deal. If I don't know who I am, it's going to affect me because I'll feel insecure in my own skin. If I don't believe in myself and I find someone throwing racist comments at me, it's going to affect me. When I was a young teenager it affected me because I was learning about myself. I was bullied, so when someone called me names, it hurt my feelings. I wish my parents had done a better job of teaching us how to express ourselves, but that's something I had to learn on my own eventually. Talking to other people of color and understanding how they handled it helped. I learned that the most important thing is that I'm okay with me. My skin color is part of who I am. If I'm okay with my insecurities it doesn't matter what they're saying to me. What matters is how I handle it."

How do some of us get to these places internally, where we are "okay" with this? It could be taking on the weight of the world at times or it could be allowing that to wash off our backs, but where does that pliancy come from? Praveen says that his upbringing assisted him with gaining wisdom, growing spiritually, and also learning how to be a human being on this earth. It helped him recognize his weaknesses more than his strengths. Praveen was raised by a mother who was religiously driven so his relationship with religion and God was driven by fear and guilt. Then, on the other hand, his dad was very cool and very loving, but also had certain problems. Although Praveen's father was very artistic, creative, loved music, and loved to sing, when he blew up, he blew up. As Praveen got older, he started to understand himself more. "Instead of just ghosting myself and pretending that I was this person, I worked very hard to be an honest person, honest with my character and my personality. Now, did that help me choose my career? Not one single bit. But it helped me become a better clinician." How we get to some of these places of resilience has to do with a conscious effort, as well as true and honest reflection on ourselves. The result of that kind of self-reflection is what needs to go back into our world and our social systems.

Praveen reflects on his experience as an inpatient mental health practitioner and says he never had a racial experience in all his 19 years working there. He takes care to captivate his clients with his words so that his race does not even come to their mind when speaking with him. He states, "I don't want them to think of me as a person of color, I just want them to appreciate that this is my color." In all of the trials and tribulations that get us to our destined practice settings, as OT practitioners, we all have that one story that made it all worth it. For Praveen, this is his:

> "We were the same age, in our 40s, but she was at an end stage in her condition of ALS [Amyotrophic Lateral Sclerosis], so she was in a hospice. When I went to see her, she was lying on the corner of the bed with an oxygen mask and her hands in splints. I introduced myself and her demeanor towards me was 'just another clinician.' You know, she was on that schedule of different OTs and PTs coming and going, just routine for her, 'What are you going to do for me?' So, we started talking and I couldn't help but look at the whole person in the sense of what was going on with her. My gut feeling gave me these vibes of anxiety; she was getting a lot of anxiety. So, I asked her, 'What are your goals?' She said, 'Well, I don't really know what my goals are because I'm in a hospice.' I said, 'Okay.' She told me that she did this and that and that her husband took care of things, otherwise it was tough. I said, 'Can I ask you about anxiety? Do you have anxiety?' She said, 'Yeah, I do.' So, I went down the symptoms of anxiety. I was thinking, why even bother with this, it doesn't matter, this is home health, but I couldn't help myself."

His instinct was to ask about her anxiety. She began to connect with him and tell him more about her symptoms. He suggested to her that maybe the anxiety was coming from an inability to express herself. Despite her limited life expectancy, Praveen believed she still had room for positive thinking. He believed that her anxiety was like a closure of doors, a blocking of the mind, where you're just instilling a lot of negative thinking. He introduced the patient to The Anxiety Cycle. Anxiety presents differently, but in general is principled in worrying about a potential threat. The patient loved it. "She said, 'Oh my gosh, no one has ever talked to me about this, the cycle.' I thought, really? She started expressing how scared she was and about ALS and where she was going in life." Praveen saw her for that visit on a Monday, then returned again on a scheduled visit a couple of days later, on Wednesday. The patient expressed how grateful she was and that she had already felt better about her anxiety. "She told me that despite being on oxygen, she had started meditating." During that Wednesday session, Praveen asked her directly what she was afraid of, what was the essence of her fear. "She said to me, 'How's my husband going to live without me? How are my kids going to live without me?'" She wasn't able to do much, had adult kids, but she just didn't know how everyone was going to live without her.

> "She said to me, 'There's nothing I can leave with them, look at me.' I said, 'Okay, you know what, I'm going to give you some suggestions. I want you to get a journal, and I want you to start writing. I want you to write a bunch of things. I want you to write your favorite movie, your favorite songs, I want you to cut out pictures from a magazine and find something that's meaningful to you and start writing. Maybe it's a picture of a sunset from a vacation. I want you to write your favorite recipes. I want you to write stories about events that happened in your life with you and your husband, your kids. The fights you guys had; the intimacy you guys had.' She took her hand and wobbled it. I said, 'Oh shoot, I'm so sorry. You can't write.' I looked at the husband. 'Okay, yes, YOU can write. Okay, your husband is the pencil, he's the tool. He's going to write for you.' I looked at him and I said, 'You cannot ask any questions; whatever she says, you write.' Then I looked at her and said, 'This is something you're going to leave behind.'"

The patient and her husband started the project immediately. When Praveen went for his next visit, a couple days later, on the Friday, the patient had managed to finish an entire journal and start a second one. In the journals were photographs that they took and she had begun writing notes in there. There were recipes, songs, clips of song lyrics. She wrote stories about her kids. She wrote about Thanksgiving moments in 1980, family gatherings, milestones, a life's worth of experiences and beautiful memories.

> "Her affect was different; she was energized, she was engaging. Also, her everyday tasks were so fluid in what she was doing because it was meaningful to her and her husband. As I was saying goodbye after that Friday visit, her husband said, 'Thank you so much! I mean, she's just a different person, we're like wife and husband again. We reminisced about our marriage and our honeymoon. It took us back to our role as wife and husband, instead of my role as a caregiver and her role as a patient.' This was a beautiful therapeutic experience for me. I loved working with this patient. I got a call on the Sunday night, the day before my next scheduled visit, and her husband said he just wanted me to know that his wife had passed away. It broke my heart; I started crying. He said, 'I just want you to know that you changed our lives, her life. As a matter of fact, she wrote you a note in the journal, and she said, *I was full of life, I was alive, when I died. Thank you.*'"

This patient changed Praveen. She reminded him to assess and see the whole person, that she was a fellow human who was scared and needed someone to talk to. Praveen continues to reflect on that patient and all the lessons he continues to learn from her. He emphasizes our need to treat the condition, but to not forget to connect with the person. You will impact a person if you go a little bit above what you're supposed to do. All Praveen did was ask about her anxiety.

REFLECTION QUESTIONS

1. Praveen powerfully explains, "I don't want them to think of me as a person of color, I just want them to appreciate that this is my color." What do you think he means by this?
2. Have you had an experience with a patient that helped you understand your "why"? What lesson(s) did this person teach you?
3. Why do you think it is important for the growth of our profession, to understand the culture of our students?

References

Berdhal, J.A. & Min, J.-A. (2012). Prescriptive stereotypes and workplace consequences for East Asians in North America. *Cultural Diversity and Ethnic Minority Psychology*, 18(2), 141–152.

Gritzer, G. & Arluke, A. (1985). *The Making of Rehabilitation*. Los Angeles, CA: University of California Press.

Mindwell (2024) *The vicious cycle of anxiety.* Retrieved from https://www.mindwell-leeds.org.uk/myself/exploring-your-mental-health/anxiety/the-vicious-cycle-of-anxiety.

Chapter 10

Practice with Integrity

ERICA V. HERRERA

"I am Kim from Reading, Pennsylvania. This is Reading spelled R.E.A. and D. as on the monopoly board, the Reading railroad, and the original outlets in the United States. I identify myself really as a mother, a grandmother, a sister, a friend, and I say that compassionately. I identify myself really, as a loyal friend."

Kim is proud of where she is from but she also knows, deeply, who she is and what she stands for. As we all search for purpose and meaning throughout our lifetime, it is comforting to know that many, like Kim, have achieved it. As occupational therapists, we are armed with meaning and purpose as tools to use daily, as we attempt to influence, habilitate, and rehabilitate our patient populations. The question is, how about us as therapists? It has been proposed that meaningful occupations enhance a positive self-identity (Phelan & Kinsella, 2009). This does not just go for those receiving occupational therapy services but also for OT practitioners. What can be more meaningful than a career of service? In Kim's case, her service started out with the US Army, along with her two brothers. She would have stayed longer if it hadn't been for her mother becoming sick. "My mother at the time was diagnosed with ischemic cardiomyopathy. My two brothers, who were still in the army, were all headed for careers based in the military. I got out because of her and I don't regret a moment of that." Kim's parents were married for 48 years prior to

Kim's mother's passing. Kim recalls, "My mom died in August, seven days before my birthday, and my father died seven weeks after her. It's crazy, you can never prepare yourself for death."

The value which Kim places on her family, friends, and other close relationships is priceless. Relationships of any kind have a profound effect on who we are, how we represent ourselves, as well as the state of our emotional and spiritual well-being. When an event happens to disrupt the relationships we hold dear, a part of us has to find a way to mend, a way to cope or attempt to make sense of the reason for the trauma. "It was very interesting to watch, you know, your parents literally slip away from you, but I processed it, I mourned her before she actually died." Having to support her young daughter, Kim had to look for her next career path.

Kim had a few injuries from the military but was still able to do rehabilitation when she was out. This sparked her interest in physical therapy. However, Kim reports, "I did not qualify because of my own injuries, so they said, 'What about occupational therapy?' I said, 'What about it? What is that?' I went and I did some volunteer work at the local hospital in my hometown." As Kim's interest in occupational therapy started to grow, she was hit with a reckoning. "I realized that my sister, my only baby sister, used to get occupational therapy and physical therapy until she was about 22. No one really talked about therapy. It's not like it is now, we know she had therapy, but that's it." Kim had to find out for herself just exactly what occupational therapy looked like.

More unfortunate incidents happened in Kim's family that assisted her in truly seeing what an OT practitioner does. Her close cousin, whom she describes as a "sister," was hit by a car, and ended up in a coma. After her godfather retired, he had a series of strokes and that's when she really got to experience occupational therapy. "They used to have PT and OT and that's when I really experienced it. I did my volunteer work and I watched them. I really was sold at that point." Kim applied to a school with an OT program in Philadelphia but she did not get in the first time. Kim explains, "It wasn't because I didn't have the GPA. I applied to a different school and didn't get in either. But I didn't want to leave far from home because I had a young child to consider, as well as where she would go to school. So, I applied again to one of the schools in Philadelphia and I got in the second time." Perplexed by this sudden admission change, Kim found out more information.

> "When I got into the school in Philadelphia they told me that I was part of Affirmative Action. It's like wait, what? So, I and a very good friend (we're still friends to this day) were part of the Affirmative Action. The Chair at the time, when we were starting off in the initial classes, shared that. She also said, 'You know, not to be mean or anything to the other people's class of 25, but there were only two people of color in all the classes in the city of Philadelphia.'"

Affirmative Action is a policy that was thought up by the late President John F. Kennedy, in the 1960s. It was originally started to end discrimination in work environments. Shortly after the assassination of Martin Luther King Jr., it made its way into the educational system. Since then, Affirmative Action has been used to assist minority and "underrepresented" students in entering prestigious institutions that they may otherwise not have been given the chance to be considered for (Hartocollis, 2022). Since its origin, this issue has been fought on both sides of the idealized spectrum, heavily. What is not up for debate is the profound impact it has had in the opportunities provided to people of color, which had not been available before its inception. It's often inferred that it is only about race, and that does have a large influence, but it has also had a profound impact for women as well. Women of all races, to be forthright. Many scholars suggest that white women have more higher education and grew to become a large part of the workforce as a result of Affirmative Action policies. In 2023, the US Supreme Court struck down Affirmative Action admissions policies (Guynn, 2023).

Kim respected the Chair of her new school. "She was from 'the city.' I would say she was from Jersey. She was down for the middle-man and for the underdog. She let the rest of the class know 'Yes, they are from that' but she also let them know that we were qualified to be there as well." Kim still found it strange that she got in because of Affirmative Action the second time, considering all that she had done. Kim explains, "I did all my prerequisites at the school, I had an associate's degree from a college in Texas, I was in the military, and I had more sciences too. My GPA, then, was a 3.9, so it wasn't as if I couldn't get in." With a start like this, it is amazing that she finished and became the clinician she is today. The adversity was expected but more important was how she responded to it. "I wasn't mad about being a part of Affirmative Action, because at the time, I went to a school that was ranked third in the nation. I always look at it like this: you do what you do. I know that, for me and the way I believe, God is going to open the door for me. However, he opens it, I'm going to get in." Kim and another female classmate of hers were the only people of color in their entire cohort. Kim found it to be very ironic.

> "I'm from Berks County, Pennsylvania, which is kind of Pennsylvania Dutch, okay. I was in my hometown, so there were Puerto Ricans, African Americans, and just white people. Even though there were a lot of minorities, we were still the minority. The school, the health science school, and all the medical schools were in the heart of North Philly; it was in the hood. It was my perception that people came into the city to get their education and then planned to leave because there was nobody in the community like them. Even my classmates, nobody kept in contact after they'd got their degrees."

Occupational therapy school for Kim was not easy. Many of Kim's professors were authors at the time, but these advanced credentials did not assist in the support of Kim's academic career. She describes how obtaining study groups was hard and she even had experiences where her professors were, in her words, "mean." Kim isn't sure if it was because she was in her 30s when she attended OT school, but it was clearly more than that. "Even when I just asked about studying, nobody wanted to study with us." It was so sad for Kim that at times she wanted to give up. True to Kim's strong foundations and her love for family, her godmother was available to help.

"My godmother, who is deceased now, and I talked a lot. I remember telling her I just really wanted to quit. She used to call me Kimberlin. I'd say my name is Kim not Kimberlin. But she'd tell me that I couldn't give up. She used to give me a lot of scriptures to read and she'd pray with me."

Although this support helped Kim to obtain her bachelor's in occupational therapy, she still had the same kind of experiences as she continued her doctoral studies later in life. The best description she gave for her experience was "passive racism." Kim further acknowledges that "it exists in education, higher education, and healthcare. It exists everywhere. I was shocked, but not shocked." Stories referring to microaggressions are described at length in this book and it's safe to say we all have probably been on the predatory side of this. Who knows everything about everyone's culture? What every person in their respective regions prefers to be called or identified as? Or how about the order in which to address a group of people without causing offense? None of us do. It may be best to just listen and welcome awareness in order to avoid the cycles of the past, especially when it comes to occupational therapy.

However, there was one highlight during the time Kim was in OT school. It may not have been directly connected to the actual program but it still brought a moment of joy for Kim.

"I did have one other relationship that I forged on the main campus. It was with a young man who lived about 30 miles outside my hometown in a more rural area. He was 'vanilla' and we really hit it off! We would hang out a lot. I think that we connected in a way because he had a different sexual orientation. He was an outlier."

It is interesting that outliers find other outliers in times of support and community. When there doesn't initially seem to be anything to connect over, there sometimes is a bond, knowing you are both different, together (i.e. the enemy of my enemy is my friend). Humans want togetherness and belonging, however they can get it. It is a way to feed the soul, even when a pairing may not make sense to the outside eye.

When Kim graduated and began to practice as an OT, she started in specialties for sentimental reasons. "My specialty was spinal cord and head trauma. I did that because of my godfather and cousin. He had so many strokes right, and my cousin who was hit by the car was a classic TBI [patient with traumatic brain injury]." Kim's first job was working for Easterseals in the District of Columbia as a contract therapist. After she did that for about a year she started to do home health. In this setting, she requested to see those who had suffered strokes and traumatic brain injuries as well. She also asked to see those who had been in car accidents. By doing so, she was seeing a lot more children. She ended up working with a company that only serviced children and stayed there for ten years. Kim says, "I really enjoy being an OT, I'm very passionate about what I do." Occupational therapists are unique in that they can have a range of skills that allow them to work in so many different specialties yet still be in the same profession. With the diverse set of experiences, what does OT mean to Kim?

> "My job is to help individuals participate in life and activities that are purposeful for them, and that actually have meaning. If you are a mother, if you are a sister, if you work at a bank as a teller, if you're a cook or chef, how is it that I can help you participate in that activity? I just try to keep it really simple, so that people can understand it."

The later part of Kim's career has been focused on pediatrics, in school-based OT. Kim has a profound love for what she does. "I have really good patient interactions." When it comes to additional stakeholders such as parents, other clinicians, or those in higher educational positions that were involved with her clients, she has had some challenging times. Kim's first negative experience came in the late 1990s. She was working for a school system and one of the special education teachers, who was also her supervisor, told her that she would be going "west of the park" to a place called "Rock Creek Park." This was a specialty school for children who had disabilities. Kim explains, "DC is divided into quadrants and there is a park that divides the city somewhat. I had no idea what the park was. I was thinking, 'What is the park and what's west of it?'" Kim realized that the school was located uptown. "It was a whole lot different. I called my parents because I was in complete disbelief that people lived like this in the same city. You also have to remember we were coming off the crack epidemic. So, I had been in other parts of the city and now I was in uptown, Northwest and you're talking about million-dollar homes."

It must have been quite a shock to have been familiar with a place and not even realize such an oasis in the city existed, especially considering the side that was known and the struggles during and after the crack epidemic. In a recent article regarding health and history in DC, it was noted that the crack epidemic reigned from the 1980s to the 1990s (King *et al.*, 2022) and in light of residential segregation, Black residents were particularly vulnerable to the epidemic. As the War on Drugs campaign became popular, the Anti-Drug Abuse Act was passed in 1986, leading to unfair sentencing practices affecting Black males disproportionately. You could be arrested with a minimum charge of five years for possession of 5 grams of crack or 500 grams of powder cocaine. This was an era of significant racial disparity in numbers of those being incarcerated. It had a profound effect on families. The trauma endured by loved ones impacted generations of people. Having this background knowledge, Kim was very shocked that such differences could exist in the same city. Kim's new working location seemed to be a good fit, with the immediate staff taking a liking to her. Yet, one negative experience came with one of the parents.

"He was a young boy – he might have been in the fourth or fifth grade – and he had a genetic disorder. His parents were older parents, meaning they were in their 50s when they had him. I wanted to get a feel for his writing skills, so I made a comment. I asked him if he practiced over the summer and I said, 'You can do better than that.' I didn't know that his feelings were hurt by what I said. His mother called as I was driving back to the office at the school to start home-schooling. She went on and on and then the dad got on the phone. He was the editor for *The Washington Post* at the time and he told me I was a piss poor excuse for an occupational therapist. So, I hung the phone up!"

When Kim arrived back at the office she was asked by her supervisor what happened. Instead of asking Kim to clarify what happened, the supervisor was immediately accusatory. She replied, "I'm not doing that and they're not going to insult me. I should stay on the phone and take that? No, we're not doing any of that." Kim was pleased that her supervisor then backed her 100%, just as she and others would many times with different authoritative challenges that arose during Kim's time there. Kim recalled so many times where there were challenges and she had to represent herself professionally and with the facts. There was an incident with one of Kim's clients where the mother did not believe Kim, she believed the clinical pediatric OT. Kim kept trying to explain that clinical and educational OT practices are completely different and that it had no place in the current matter, but the mother would not listen. At one of the large staff meetings with the mother, the mother's attorney showed up.

"He threw his tape recorder on the table and they were scared of him. I thought, who the heck is this fool acting like this? I asked if he was recording and he said, 'Yes.' I said, 'Well you didn't ask me if you could record me. If you're going to record, then you need my permission, and I believe everyone else at the table also.' There was a vice principal at the table, the head of the department, but everyone was afraid. I pride myself in understanding the law. There are certain things that you cannot pull over me because I love what I do. And I love the children in the school system. He was just kind of shocked, thinking, wait a minute, who is this chocolate lady with all this attitude? He was still nasty, but he backed down. He did try to challenge me a couple times in the meeting and I told him, 'You practice law and I practice OT. We can come together, we can agree to disagree, or we can come together and agree.'"

The number of complex interactions in day-to-day life for anyone are endless. However, it takes a special kind of character to handle the types of interactions Kim has dealt with throughout her career, especially considering the area where she works, her populations of interest, and what she physically looks like. Of course, in a perfect world the physical appearance of the OT practitioner should not matter, but it does. Kim has put in all the study, research, and countless hours just so that the kids in her school-based system can thrive. Thankfully her heart has always been with the kids. Not all of Kim's challenges have been interracial power complexes; sometimes these microaggressions come from patients or colleagues who are not white.

> "I had a home health patient and he was African American. I called to set up my time prior to getting to the door. I don't know who opened the door but it wasn't him because he couldn't come to the door. So, I walk around and he's looking at me like, who are you? I said, 'I'm Kim, the OT. I told you, remember?' He said, 'I didn't talk to you?' I told him, 'Yes.' He said, 'Come over here,' so I went closer. He told me, 'You sound like a white girl.' I said, 'Oh.'"

Kim's career and life experiences are a lesson in adversity.

> "I have created who I am based on the work that I do. I feel that you should always practice with integrity. Be your authentic self. I am first a woman, I am a Black woman, I am an educated Black woman and I stand proudly on the shoulders of my ancestors. So, I don't hold or take anything that I have lightly. I do it to make them proud. I mean 'them' as in those before me and my parents, who pushed us to succeed in higher education. I do take that very seriously. I'm not a nasty person, but I don't mind being challenged. I'm reaping the reward. Because it doesn't matter what you believe in. If you believe in the Bible, if you believe in Confucius or Buddha, if you believe in the Torah or the Quran or if you just believe in the universe, whatever you put out there is what you get back."

REFLECTION QUESTIONS

1. Why is it important to know that microaggressions can be intentional or unintentional?

2. Which of your identities (e.g. race, language, religion, gender, sexuality) could lead you to unintentionally commit a microaggression?
3. What factors can lessen or increase the impact of microaggressions on an individual?

References

Guynn, J. (2023). White Women Benefit Most from Affirmative Action. So Why do They Oppose it? USA TODAY. Retrieved from: www.usatoday.com/story/money/2023/06/29/affirmative-action-who-benefitswhite-women/70371219007.

Hartocollis, A. (2022). How the term "affirmative action" came to be. *New York Times*, Oct. 31, 2022. Retrieved from: www.nytimes.com/2022/10/31/us/politics/affirmative-action-history.html.

King, C.J., Buckley, B.O., Maheshwari, R., & Griffith, D.M. (2022). Race, place, and structural racism: A review of health and history in Washington, D.C. *Health Affairs*, 41(2). Retrieved from: www.healthaffairs.org/doi/10.1377/hlthaff.2021.01805.

Phelan, S.K. & Kinsella, E.A. (2009). Occupational identity: Engaging socio-cultural perspectives. *Journal of Occupational Science*, (16)2, 85–91.

Chapter 11

A Mestizo of Self-Discovery

ALAA ABOU-ARAB

Mixed-race or multiracial individuals in the US represent approximately 7% of its population; this number is likely to continue increasing (Davenport *et al.*, 2021). Because race is a social construct, racial identity is fluid and can change throughout a person's life. A study by the Pew Research Center found that three in ten adults with a multiracial identity have changed how they describe their race over the years (Parker *et al.*, 2015). For US Latinxs, being mixed race takes on an even deeper meaning. As described by Bonifacio (2022):

> As Latinx immigrants, our subjectivities, what we call ourselves and how we see each other, intersect with Black–White dichotomies in the US and the colorism and pigmentocracies contrived in our natal countries. We are re-racialized in the diaspora, forced to check a box that we don't understand, and contribute to the machinery of anti-blackness. (p.75)

For Pamela, it has been a process of self-discovery. "I am a Colombian woman; I identify as mestiza." The term *mestizo/a* means "mixed" in Spanish. A product of European conquest and colonization, it is predominantly used to describe individuals with a mixed ancestry of White European and Indigenous background and sometimes enslaved Africans and their descendants (Rodriguez Mega, 2021). However, mestizo claims multiple meanings throughout Latin

American history. On the one hand, it was used by Spanish and Portuguese colonizers to classify the blend of ethnicities into a hierarchical ethno-racial caste system. On the other hand, it was used by governments across Latin America to disguise campaigns of *blanqueamiento* (whitening) to "dilute" the African and Indigenous ancestry of their populations through a rhetoric of harmonious racial integration (Rodriguez Mega, 2021).

As a Colombian immigrant who only thought about herself as "Colombian," Pamela was racialized as a white Latina by default on entering the United States. "As long as I don't talk, I get identified as white, and I benefit from that." Once she opens her mouth and begins to speak, her accent signifies her Latina identity in the US. As such, her social transit as a US citizen in the country has been marked by a constant need to reclaim her multiracial background and understand the colonial wound of her identity as a mestiza, thinking about it as sociologist Silvia Rivera Cusicanqui (2018) suggests, as an emancipatory social category that can host a dialogue among her ancestries.

Her journey into occupational therapy and as an occupational therapist is mixed with a plethora of emotions and accomplishments. She comes from what she describes as a "wealthy background" in Colombia. She was raised in the arts; her dad is an architect, and her mom is a visual artist, and she thrived in those areas. Pamela wanted to study film. "I wanted to study film because I wanted to be a war reporter." When the opportunity came to begin her university education, she had a chance to attend a public university with a full scholarship. At that time, her dad's firm had gone bankrupt, and the country was in sociopolitical turmoil and economic recession. The school offered film studies but also had OT, which, until then, was not on her radar. She noticed that the OT courses integrated medical science, anthropology, biology, and the arts, and she thought, "This is what I really want; it sounds like me." She felt that by pursuing an OT degree, she would be able to do something more tangible in her country. Unlike OT school in the US, where most students come from a middle to upper socioeconomic background, she was one of the few who came from relative wealth. "The majority of my classmates were from a lower socioeconomic background, and I was the only bilingual student. All the literature at that time was in English, so I spent most of the time translating for professors and students." Pamela experienced much pressure early on in her OT training. One of the most challenging moments she experienced was during her field-work assignment at a shelter for the unhoused in Colombia. "One of my clients said to me that I didn't really have to speak, that just by looking at me and my mannerisms, they could tell I was never going to be a part of their community." It was a hard realization that led her to study outside Colombia.

She found herself at the University of Nebraska, in the "International Hall," where most international students resided. She might have found comradery with the other foreign-born students, but she had another realization. "I would say at least 90% of the students came from small towns in their country; I am from Bogotá, a big city." She continued with self-reflection on her identity, background, and experiences and realized, "Oh my god, I know so little about me. I grew up with this European and Americanized model of identity and education... I have been so whitewashed." This prompted her to investigate cultural issues within the profession. She moved back to Colombia after one year abroad, finished her degree, and began working as an OT. "I was a coordinator of two different social projects. One was with older adults in extreme poverty, and the other was with children with disabilities in a special education-type school." However, Colombia's social and political situation at the time made it very hard for her to practice. Her mother suggested she went abroad again. Pamela wanted to pursue education in OT further. "I knew that wherever I ended up, I wanted to work in the US first and acquire street smarts and get the context, and then go get my doctorate."

Her US occupational therapy experience began in Philadelphia, Pennsylvania. She received a work visa sponsorship from a rehabilitation company specializing in skilled nursing facilities. It was a difficult transition for her. That is not a surprise. It is an experience many in the OT workforce will never understand. Things that practitioners implicitly take for granted, such as changing jobs or seeing family, are often impossible for people on a work visa. You can imagine the anxiety this can produce. "I was just trying to keep my head above water. I didn't want to upset anyone, but I started recognizing that things were not working." While working as an OT she applied to OT school. There was no direct path to an occupational therapy doctorate (OTD) at the time; you had to have a master's degree to apply for the doctorate. That led to an unfair experience that exposed some of the inequities with the international systems in OT. Pamela already had clinical experience, but her classmates had not completed a field-work assignment yet. "They had to create a separate syllabus for me. It is so unfair how the international system in occupational therapy translates your work." The time, energy, and money spent could have been avoided. During her first year, a track was opened to those with a bachelor's degree in OT, so she was able to transition to get her post-professional OTD. By the time she finished her OTD degree, Pamela had six years of experience working in geriatrics in the US. However, it was not something she was really into. She did not have many choices due to the limitations of the work visa. While finishing her OTD, she got married to a US citizen, which allowed her to begin doing some instructional work at the university she attended and to move to a per diem role in post-acute care settings and as an independent contractor in school-based practice.

Pamela has now lived in the US for almost 20 years. Human occupation and culture are intertwined in Pamela's therapeutic approach. When she speaks, it arouses the curiosity of patients and co-workers.

"Sometimes they think I am Russian, sometimes from Spain, sometimes the Middle East. When I say I am Colombian, they sometimes respond with, 'Well, you went to school here, right?' I often just say, 'Yes, I got my doctorate in the US.' But I sometimes wonder whether if I had said, 'No, I did my education in Colombia,' I would have built that same trust."

The importance of building that relationship and bond with our patients and clients cannot be overstated. Minoritized OTs must often justify their qualifications by emphasizing their relation to the constructs of western civilization or whiteness. Pamela was a licensed and practicing clinician before ever setting foot in a US OT program. She does not have to justify that to anyone.

She now resides in Southern Arizona, just an hour north of the Mexican border, and she does not have to justify it as much. "I now have the ability to culturally relate a little bit more. I can do a full treatment and full evaluations in Spanish." Her experiences transcend not only state borders but international boarders as well. She has done work abroad in places like Cuba, Ecuador, and Guatemala as a research faculty member. One experience, written in a reference letter by a colleague of Pamela's, illustrates the significance of finding that connection between culture and occupation. She was working on a seven-year-old child's wheelchair for proper fitting and positioning. The child was crying the entire time and Pamela recognized the mom's exhaustion while trying to work on this wheelchair. Because she was one of the few bilingual individuals working on this project at the time, she could investigate the reason for the child's crying and attempt to ease the mom's stress.

"The mom did not seem interested in the wheelchair; she just wanted the child to stop crying. I asked her if maybe she was crying because the child was usually complaining of constipation...we talked about what local fruits and vegetables might be gentler on her stomach. I didn't even realize it at the time, because it was kind of automatic for me, but I really validated the mother's concerns. That is why it's so important to really attune with the local reality of not just the country, but the state, the city where you live and work."

For many immigrants or children of immigrants in the US, life can feel like two separate scenarios. Having not lived in Colombia for an extended period, Pamela feels like a stranger when she returns. That is not easy to compartmentalize. "I recognize now that I am pushing toward being the outsider; that hurts a bit; that's a part of me." Our environments, surroundings, and interpersonal relationships can change over time, as does our view of occupation, and Pamela has had a mix of all of it. Her perception of what occupation is has evolved alongside her journey of self-discovery.

Learning the US healthcare system is challenging, even for those born and raised here. The for-profit system is filled with health disparities, and rehabilitation is no different. People requiring rehabilitation across their lifespans are diverse and vulnerable. Many demographic factors contribute to these disparities, and often they co-exist with the disability we are evaluating and treating. Pamela's experiences of practicing OT internationally empower her to take on that responsibility of caring for culture in her treatment sessions, despite the healthcare system that constantly inhibits us from providing client-centered care.

> "Occupation to me is a human activity that has meaning to you and your reality. Basketball is an activity, but for some it's an occupation because it has meaning and value in their daily living... I admit, I haven't always done it this way, especially when I started practicing in the US. I worked for a company that really valued productivity levels and how much money you could extract for them. I wasn't always able to provide my patients with meaningful activity. I spent so much time giving my best for the patient to be independent in whatever they do. But we are interdependent all our life; I always wonder what the value is of what I am doing. I feel guilty about that sometimes, especially when I have to write goals.
>
> That's why I like acute care; it's basic activities of daily living, it's baby steps, and I can see the value in that. But, for example, in inpatient rehabilitation, you return to the community, and I am preparing you to go back again to the social system. If no social support is in place, I am doing you a disservice. I can make you independent, but your lack of social support and the economic and political systems are against you. What is your quality of life? That's why I go back to the cultural aspect of the way I see occupation. If we keep replicating occupations in our mind that have meaning to us as clinicians but are not meaningful to the person we're working with, we are missing the point."

Pamela has a lot of occupations and roles that she loves, such as illustrating, spending time with her family, and being outdoors. "I come alive being in the wilderness. It is a feeling of insignificance, but simultaneously being a part of everything." True to her world-view and way of life, her favorite occupation is not about her but about those special moments. "It's difficult to describe. It is difficult to explain because it happens to all of us." It goes back to why we chose to be OTs. "It could be a commode transfer from the bed, something we do all the time." It's a human relationship that cannot be overstated and is specific and unique to the OT profession. "It's a different level of connection, and it's usually a stranger. That's really what keeps me going." It might be a moment that she describes as sacred, where there is beauty in that intimate connection. She mentioned a commode transfer, but those moments could be completing a dressing task, passing a driving test, or writing your name. Pamela's empathy and humility should be replicated. "I don't think I ever stopped learning from those interactions; seeking those moments of humanity that can grow the therapeutic relationship. All the charting is essential to the system, but it doesn't replace those moments." Pamela's OT toolkit has many teaching and learning moments, moments of connection and humanity. Let her humility guide your practice in a world becoming increasingly interdependent across borders and languages. She is an amazingly experienced OT, and she is still learning.

REFLECTION QUESTIONS

1. How might you practice humility when servicing a client from a different cultural or ethnic background from your own?
2. Our identities evolve throughout our lifespan. What have your experiences been like as your identity evolves with your life experiences and cultural environments?

References

Bonifacio, A. (2022). Our patrias cannot liberate us from anti-Blackness: Post-racial myths in the Latinx diaspora. *The Black Scholar*, 52(1), 75–85.

Davenport, L.D., Iyengar, S., & Westwood, S.J. (2021). Racial identity, group consciousness, and attitudes: A framework for assessing multiracial self-classification. *American Journal of Political Science*, 66(3), 570–586.

Parker, K., Menasce Horowitz, J., Morin, R., & Lopez, M.H. (2015). *Multiracial in America*. Pew Research Center. Retrieved from: www.pewresearch.org/social-trends/2015/06/11/multiracial-in-america.

Rivera Cusicanqui, S. (2018). *Un Mundo Ch'ixi es Posible: Ensayos Desde un Presente en Crisis* [*A New World is Possible: Essays from a Present in Crisis*]. Buenos Aires: Tinta Limón.

Rodriguez Mega, E. (2021). How the mixed-race mestizo myth warped science in Latin America. *Nature*, 600(7889), 374–378. Retrieved from: www.nature.com/articles/d41586-021-03622-z.

Chapter 12

I am Proud to be an OT

ALAA ABOU-ARAB

As is talked about at length in this book, first- and second-generation occupational therapy practitioners often carry with them exceptional stories of both triumph and trauma. Mitchell's parents are both South Vietnamese and settled in Southern California after the Vietnam war. "My dad came later; he worked for the South Vietnamese government and had been captured by the North Vietnamese for a little bit." The war ended in 1975 and over the next couple of decades, over a million Vietnamese refugees settled in the United States (Harjanto & Batalova, 2021). His parents wanted to wait until they arrived in the US to start their family. His father attended college and gained employment with the local government as an eligibility worker. His mom worked as a manicurist. Mitchell continues, "I navigated that first-generation struggle, where you come home to something different than what you experience at school with white and Hispanic kids... I didn't grow up in an area where there were a lot of Asian people." It is truly a stressor and an experience that can only be lived to be understood—the moments, as a child from immigrants, where you just feel different. Imagine bringing an authentic dish to school for lunch as everyone stares at you with curiosity, or speaking one language as you're walking out the front door, then speaking another as you enter the classroom. Mitchell is an only child and always felt as if he just wanted to fit in. "Growing up as a Vietnamese American, it seemed very different from everyone else, it was kind of what defined me."

He lived a "very sheltered" life as he puts it. It wasn't until he went to college that he was able to explore his identity. Mitchell moved away for his undergraduate studies, but he still felt as if he was always thinking about his parents; they pushed him to choose a school that was close to them. "It wasn't as if I knew what I wanted to do; I went there because that's what they wanted." His college experience gave him the opportunity to learn about himself, beyond how he related to his family, and what they expected of him. Mitchell explains that he obtained employment in college, gained more independence, and realized another important piece of his identity. "I experimented in college and felt that I came to terms with being gay, which is definitely not what my parents wanted and it's not even something that we really talk about today." Mitchell had a boyfriend for a couple of years during college and when they broke up, he came out to his father. "It was the first experience I had ever had like that, and I wanted—I don't know—acceptance or something. He told me I could do whatever I wanted after he passed away... I don't even think he remembers it." He hasn't directly come out to his mother. "My mom has always been homophobic, and I just don't think she could handle it right now." Living as someone who identifies as gay and a person of color in the US is a challenge to manage and it can feel isolating. The coming-out process may require a unique approach, because coming out is a personal choice and the experience is different for everybody.

However difficult it is or will be, being a gay Vietnamese American isn't the only thing that defines him. Mitchell clarifies, "I am an OT, that's a big part of my identity... I am happy with my work, and I find a lot of pride in what I do." Mitchell finished his undergraduate degree and didn't know what he wanted to do next. He joined an AmeriCorps program called City Year, where he provided school support for teachers and did after-school programming. Mitchell admits he was afraid of the "real world" and although he was able to see an OT practitioner in the school setting, that wasn't what inspired him to become an OT practitioner. "My dad had a stroke and I actually saw an OT in the acute care setting. That was sort of my introduction." Mitchell had witnessed his friends from college jumping from job to job and he knew he wanted something stable but also something that pushed him to connect with people. He adds, "I am a very introverted person." He moved back home, took the prerequisite courses and applied to OT programs in Southern California, close to his parents. Although he didn't get into the school he wanted because of a mistake on the application, when he got the acceptance from the other school, it didn't matter, he was ready. "I was ready to move on with the next phase of my life, but OT school was actually very hard for me."

When Mitchell's father fell ill, he moved back in with his parents. He lived at home during his OT education and didn't realize how much difference that would make. "I got to become myself in under-grad... Moving back in with my parents, I was back to being who they wanted me to be." Hoping he'd have the same experiences with his peers as he did during his undergraduate experience, Mitchell was disappointed. Mitchell describes an experience not unlike other OT school experiences in the US. "It was like a private school; I think 60% of my class[mates] were white... It was a very different experience from the one I had during undergrad." Essentially, he felt he had to hide part of his identity at home and on top of that, deal with the stressors of being the "other" in graduate school. "I actually started taking antidepressants, it was just so hard for me."

Mitchell felt as though he had worked so hard to figure out who he was and suddenly had to return to the trauma of compartmentalizing his identity. Most of his faculty members were white, but there were a few faculty members he felt comfortable with. Although he was in graduate school for a health profession, he didn't feel as though the professors were helpful enough clinically. "I felt as if the experienced academicians were farther and farther away from the clinic and it wasn't representative of clinical practice." He resonated more with the instructors who were still doing clinical practice. He finished his degree and obtained his license to practice in 2019. Shortly after his career started, the global pandemic began.

Having now worked for over three years, mainly in the hospital or inpatient rehabilitation setting, his view of occupations, in a clinical sense, is ADL based. He understands that the definition and concept of occupation is bigger than a person's hygiene, dressing, and bathing.

"I know that occupation is more than that, it's about the activities that give your life meaning and I think I am still struggling to have that in my life. It's been hard, just to have something for myself that is part of my self-care." The Covid-19 pandemic revealed the burnout health-care clinicians have had to deal with. The emotional toll it takes on someone is high and with an already full plate to carry, Mitchell found himself needing to be more deliberate about his occupational balance. "It was so much easier when I was younger to go on a hike with friends, to go to the beach, now I have to be so much more intentional with the time that I have." In a recent study (Murthy, 2022), more than half of healthcare workers report symptoms of burnout and are dealing with depression, anxiety, and other challenges to their mental well-being. If we could isolate Mitchell's burnout, theoretically, it would be easier to solve. Unfortunately, many of those who are living with multiple minoritized identities don't have that privilege. The burnout is piled on to the top of their histories and experiences. Mitchell was right, he needed to be deliberate.

This consideration cannot be ignored in the workplace either. Acute and inpatient clinicians are often lifting, pulling, straining, and spend most of their days on their feet. It is physically demanding. We must practice in a biomechanically safe manner in order to avoid hurting ourselves. As individuals from marginalized backgrounds, we must also look out for ourselves in a non-physical sense. Our emotional and mental well-being shouldn't be dismissed in the workplace. Mitchell is a floater, which means he works on multiple floors and units; he isn't assigned a particular place (e.g. orthopedics, oncology, neurology). Some days can be very easy and other days not so much. His plate went from being too full, to overflowing, but he reiterates how he takes pride in his work. The acute care setting is fast and you see so many different people every day. You will treat many individuals who aren't from the same background or don't share the same experiences as you. "I work with a large Korean and Armenian population...and I try my best to find a commonality." Trying to find that common ground can be a challenge, and often occupational therapists miss the meaning of what the client or patient wants.

"As OTs, we try our best to make people as independent as they can be...and sometimes it's not what is expected from that culture." This is an example where client-centered practice is a detriment to the occupational needs of the person we are treating. Mitchell highlights the need for a more *family-centered* approach. "I get a patient who falls and breaks their hip. I am teaching them hip precautions and adaptive equipment and, honestly, they couldn't care less. They say, 'My family will take care of it.'" Mitchell could have ignored all the cultural nuances and pushed for his patient to learn how to use a reacher, a dressing stick, or a sock-aide, but his humility allowed for the patient and their family to be in the center of the intervention. Although OT practitioners should emphasize awareness and humility in patient care, having these attributes does not eliminate a clinician's bias. We all have different experiences and exposures that lead to our perception of others.

Mitchell was working in the inpatient rehab unit one morning, looking over a chart before he saw his next patient. An inpatient rehab facility or an acute rehab unit is a dedicated facility for one's rehabilitation and, unlike a hospital, its sole focus is on rehabilitation, as patients are medically stable. It's also not like a skilled nursing facility, because the patients are getting more intensive therapy, typically three hours or more per day. Mitchell had a patient who was a 40-year-old white male who was admitted to his facility following a motor vehicle accident. As he reviewed the patient's chart, he found that the patient was divorced, had two children, was drunk at the time of the incident and the accident had been his fault. "I was reading the chart, and I began to judge the patient. Oh my God, you could've killed someone." It's a common reaction from practitioners, but it does indicate a bias and could hinder the therapeutic relationship. Often, when our preconceived notions are debunked, there is growth and learning that comes from it. Mitchell continues, "He turned out to be very sweet and receptive to all the education and training we provided." The patient made great progress, and fast. Mitchell got to see him go from maximum assistance (where the patient was doing approximately 25% of the task) to 100% independence with his basic activities of daily living. This experience gave Mitchell the training he wasn't expecting. "It reminded me to always keep an open mind.

I went into it thinking, 'Here's this Wall Street bro, this is going to be awful,' but it was really special."

As a Vietnamese American gay male OT practitioner, Mitchell's story reveals a multiplicity of possibilities for defining occupation. The interrelationship between identity and occupation is ever important and should be a focus for practitioners, students, and academicians. How our patients or clients view themselves, and how we view them, has direct implications for the therapeutic relationship. What is important to the OT practitioner may not coincide with the needs of the people they serve. Mitchell defines occupation as activities that give your life meaning. He admits not doing that for himself and wants to be intentional about his self-care. "My body is my livelihood; I can't let myself get injured... How am I going to pay the bills?" Taking care of himself in a way that also fits his identity has been difficult but, as Mitchell says, it must be intentional. He has started stretching and exercising more.

When asked about his favorite occupation, Mitchell mentions going paddleboarding with friends. "I don't know if it's my favorite occupation, I've only done it once, but I really loved it." He describes the inner calmness he found being in the open water. Mitchell deserves that calmness; he deserves to live his life with meaning and reduced worry. He takes pride in being an occupational therapy practitioner who helps others find meaning in their lives. As his journey for meaning continues, we should take pride in him.

REFLECTION QUESTIONS

1. What actions are you willing to take to make someone like Mitchell feel safe and appreciated as a classmate, a colleague, and a human being?
2. What can you do now to add meaning and balance to your life in order to prevent future burnout as an OT practitioner?
3. How often in your academic career have you done something because someone else wanted you to? Do you feel this will affect your clinical decisions as a new practitioner?

References

Harjanto, L. & Batalova, J. (2021). Vietnamese Immigrants in the United States. Migration Information Source. Migration Policy Institute. Retrieved from: www.migrationpolicy.org/article/vietnamese-immigrants-united-states.

Murthy, V.H. (2022). Confronting health worker burnout and well-being. *New England Journal of Medicine*, 387, 577–579.

Chapter 13

I Was Always the Only One

ALAA ABOU-ARAB

Erica knew she always wanted or often needed to be in the medical field, but she wasn't quite sure where she would fit in this area. She grew up in a Northern California household, with a mother of Nigerian descent who spent much of her younger days between Nigeria and London, England. Her father, a Black American, was born in Chicago and raised in California. As the oldest child of three, she did her best to make sure everyone was taken care of and provided with the security she didn't have. She witnessed drug use and domestic violence in her home and that shaped her worldview. "I mean, looking back at it, you know, I'm glad I went through what I went through, but it wasn't the greatest," she states. It was never about her, and through prayer, she found occupational therapy. During her admissions interview, the professor conducting the interview had a research focus on domestic violence in occupational therapy. Erica didn't believe it was a coincidence, to her it was God.

Research suggests that students of color in occupational therapy education are not shielded from marginalization and racism (Lucas, 2017). For Erica, being a Black woman in a white-dominated field, this is how it always was. She was the *only* Black student in her kindergarten class and, many years later, the *only* Black student in her graduate school occupational therapy class. While attending OT school, she knew other students of color, but no one like her. There wasn't anyone who looked like her in the department.

"You might not always acknowledge it, but you still feel it. I would feel it when we would get on to the topic of culture or diet; I felt as if I was by myself. My classmates would make assumptions about the people in the case studies we would go over in class. They would judge the clients on how they feed their kids and shop for them, and other life choices. I would often be the only one trying to look at the culture and overall big picture of the person. We live in a county where there are single-parent households, where the parent works two jobs, and has three to four kids. You have to put yourself in the life of that individual, and see that maybe that person is doing the best they can."

Despite the lack of Black faculty and students within her OT department, Erica found support outside the OT department. The assistant pastor was a Black woman from the islands and a higher-level faculty member was a Black man. She didn't need the motivation, she had that on her own, but it was nice for her to see that representation in higher education. Often, being the only Black person in your classroom or clinic can place an extra amount of pressure on you to perform. Not for Erica. "Sadly, I was prepared for it, and by the time I got to my master's program, I was almost numb to it," she says. Erica expected to be the only one and when she wasn't, it surprised her. "That's weird! How come there are so many Black people here?" This type of normalization of the minority experience—of being othered—can mean that we see ourselves through the majority population lens and we navigate the world as if we are the only minoritized person in the environment.

Erica is currently a certified hand therapist, but before she took on this role, she worked as a traveling occupational therapist for a year after graduation. Most of her traveling experience was in the Midwest of the US.

"I grew up as a traveling OT. I wouldn't be the therapist I am today without that experience as a traveler. I've had people say racist things to my face. Not like California racism, where it's like, 'I am so sorry, we forgot to tell you the meeting was 6 o'clock.'"

Overt, explicit racism and microaggressions from patients who are relying on her for care can be overwhelming and difficult to navigate. Unfortunately, this is not an uncommon situation as research indicates that Black professionals are more likely than any other racial group to face microaggressions and discrimination. Furthermore, Black professionals have less access to mentorship than their white counterparts (Cheeks, 2018; Brewton-Johnson, 2021). It was these experiences that led Erica to find out what kind of OT she wanted to be. It also shaped how she approaches her interventions, even in a setting where many might not think culture or race are important. "Hand therapy and upper extremity rehabilitation can be so specific." For Erica, it is always more than a hand injury. "Who am I really seeing? Who am I working with? Is it an athlete with a finger fracture, a new mom with a fractured finger, or a woman in her 80s who hasn't had a single injury in her entire life?" Erica can see the importance and power of culture. "I feel as if I deal with race and culture all day long, because...I am choosing to not ignore it. I need to meet them where they are." For Erica, culture often plays a larger role for her than race. Not all minorities are a monolith and for her it is important to distinguish that. Being the daughter of Black parents from different continents and cultures, she can see the significant role of culture within race. "You can be a Black [person] from Minnesota and never know anything about cooking in the South." Her personal and professional experiences led to this confidence and her ability to see every patient holistically.

The American Occupational Therapy Association's 2019 Workforce and Salary Survey indicated that Black or African Americans made up 3% of occupational therapists and occupational therapy assistants in the United States and indicated that women account for over 90% of OT clinicians (American Occupational Therapy Association 2020). However, for Erica as a Black woman, the trauma from microaggressions came from a multitude of directions. She shares a story of how this manifested in the clinic. "I had a young white male with severe anxiety." It was quite noticeable to Erica on his first visit. "He was looking everywhere, frantic, and he was rocking and looking down." Erica asked him if he was alright and the patient quickly responded, "There are so many women here, I just can't do it, there are so many women." Erica attempted to redirect the patient to the task and begin her evaluation. The patient was being seen for hand pain due to Ehlers-Danlos syndrome, a connective tissue disorder. The patient continued to perseverate on his inability to work in the environment with so many women, which included patients and OT practitioners.

The patient requested to move to a different, more private location. Erica chose an area that wasn't entirely closed off but private enough to continue the session safely. Despite efforts to communicate her discomfort, Erica continued to treat him for eight to ten sessions. She explains, "These were the worst [sessions]... I have never had to use so much of my mental health training, until that moment. The patient would say things like, 'I just want to kill myself; I hate myself' or 'I hate women.'" Despite the patient's explicit bias toward women, he persisted to have Erica be his therapist. "This wasn't even a Black and white thing, this was gender. I'm like, you know, your therapist is a woman." This difficult navigation between treating the patient with equity and putting oneself in harm's way is not an uncommon occurrence with occupational therapists. "Day after day, it was this abuse to me. He would curse me out." Erica didn't even realize the amount of abuse she was enduring and even her co-workers didn't realize how bad it was. "I felt supported when my team found out how bad it was. The whole department worked together to figure out a resolution." These experiences aren't uncommon, and even in the midst of direct danger and lack of safety, Erica persisted because that's what she'd always done.

> "You're the only Black person in school, or the only Black person at the market that day, so you build this skin as if you're supposed to take it...and you prevail, you get your degree, or whatever it is you are trying to accomplish. But it's not okay today. I am tired. Instead of being the Black girl, can I just be the girl? Even Superman gets to just be Clark Kent."

The expectations placed on Black women in the workplace are

incredibly unfair. Erica says that she had never felt misogyny or direct discrimination because of her gender until her experience with this patient.

That story occurred on the West Coast, in what's commonly known as a thoroughly diverse and socially liberal part of the US. Yet Erica didn't feel she had the protections required for her to safely provide treatment for that patient. She recounts a story of her time in the Midwest, a place a lot less diverse and more socially conservative, that truly indicates the power of occupation, even as the only Black woman—again. Erica was working in a skilled nursing facility, treating a white woman in her 70s, who came in following a hospitalization due to complications from a urinary tract infection (UTI). It is common for individuals with a UTI to get generally weak and deconditioned and with a combination of antibiotics and rehabilitation, patients tend to make a full recovery. "She was getting better, then I noticed that she was having issues with her hands." This was before Erica became a hand specialist. "I was looking for opportunities [to learn about hands], and I didn't know why her hands were becoming [so] swollen. This was out of my realm of practice, but I suggested to her and her husband that they mention it next time her physician came by."

Unfortunately, the patient's condition worsened, and this was especially difficult for the patient's husband. "It was really shocking...he thought it was something she could recover from." Erica persisted as she always has, continuing the treatments and setting goals for the patient to engage in meaningful activities. "Let's just keep going. Try your normal routine as much as possible, allowing her to continue being her...as much as possible." The relationship grew with both the patient and her husband, and they only wanted to have Erica as their occupational therapist. One morning, Erica went to see this patient first. "I remember it being sort of intimate... It was the holiday season, so there weren't a lot of staff and there was snow on the ground." She escorted her patient from her room to the rehabilitation gym and began the session.

The patient's functional performance had declined and she needed an assistive device for mobility. They completed the session, which the patient tolerated well, and Erica began to take her back to her room. "She was telling me some of her favorite Christmas stories and I was sharing some of mine, and then on the loudspeaker a song started playing. She started humming it and then I started humming it...and then she took the high and I took the low, so we were singing this Christmas song together." As they approached the patient's room, there was silence and the patient stated, "That was really nice," and Erica replied, "Yes, it was." Erica continued with the rest of her day, attended to the rest of her patients, and left to return the following day. She went to this patient first, as she has done so many times before. "I went to get her that morning, and they told me that she had passed away." The emotional trauma of losing a patient is immeasurable. Occupations are fluid and take different forms as the environment and contexts change. In that moment before she passed, they came together in an occupational cohesiveness, and they shared a song. Moments like these are scattered throughout this book, showing the power of occupation and human connection.

Erica was able to navigate the diverse contexts of occupational therapy and thrive in it. "I try to pray for everything, about everything, and every decision." She is a certified hand therapist, professor, and researcher, and her career has ascended. Her strong faith and conviction to improve the lives of others through occupation should be celebrated. In 2022, the United States Senate confirmed the country's first African American woman to serve on the Supreme Court. This is undoubtedly an outstanding achievement, but the racism and misogyny experienced by the judge, not just during the confirmation but throughout her lifespan, bears witness to the experiences of many others in this country who have not reached the pinnacle of their careers, as she has. The resiliency is palpable, and it is simultaneously unfortunate that she needed to be this resilient. Erica, with God at her side, perseveres, despite having been the only one, and imagines an equitable world.

REFLECTION QUESTIONS

1. Within your journey to OT school or as an OT practitioner, reflect on a moment where you made a connection with a client/patient. How did this impact you as a person? As a student/practitioner?
2. What does the following line mean to you?: "Often culture plays a larger role for her than race. Not all minorities are a monolith."
3. Professionally or personally, are there things that you feel you are now "numb" to and accept the wrongful treatment just so you can move on and get through your day? What are they?

References

American Occupational Therapy Association (2020). *AOTA 2019 Workforce and Salary Survey*. Retrieved from: https://library.aota.org/AOTA-Workforce-Salary-Survey-2019.

Brewton-Johnson, M. (2021). Working as a young, Black woman in America. Harvard Business Review. Retrieved from: https://hbr.org/2021/03/working-as-a-young-black-woman-in-america.

Cheeks, M. (2018). How Black women describe navigating race and gender in the workplace. Harvard Business Review. Retrieved from: https://hbr.org/2018/03/how-black-women-describe-navigating-race-and-gender-in-the-workplace?ab=at_art_art_1x1.

Lucas, C.B. (2017). *Occupational Therapists of Color: Perceptions of the Academic Experience*. (Publication No. 10276527). Doctoral dissertation, Johnson & Wales University. ProQuest Dissertations Publishing.

Chapter 14

Hey, My Name is Alaa, I'm Your OT Today

ERICA V. HERRERA

"My name is short for Aladdin." Alaa graciously shares his full name, as he recalls the difficulties he faced on a day-to-day basis when providing occupational therapy interventions to patients in an acute care setting. He provides further education by explaining, "Alaa means excellence and elevation and the second part 'din,' pronounced '*deen*' means religion. It means someone of a high religious standard, or nobility of faith. I never went by that, my entire life." How much does one's name matter? According to Zulu (2017), who was the founder and senior editor for the journal *Africology*, it not only matters, but it is a way of preserving culture and identity. Zulu's work highlights the issues surrounding enslaved African Americans in the US. He explains that when it comes to the name of an individual, however, having that name is a basic human right that is shared by all. Zulu points out that people around the world have been burdened by the adoption of European names. In turn, by taking on a name that is not your own, your identity becomes second to the name which you portray. This problem is not new for Alaa. His name is often mistaken for Allah or the Arabic word for God.

"I've been getting it all day, every day, ever since I was a kid. 'Where are you from?' 'When did you move here?' 'Your name is God?'

It's relentless. And people will pronounce it a thousand different ways. Some elongate the A in the beginning of my name, so it sounds like 'Aaaaaala,' or they stretch the end of the name, so it sounds like 'Alaaaaa.' Without knowing a single thing about me, except for my name, assumptions about my faith, my culture, and my interests are made. I've had it from my patients, from colleagues, classmates, you name it."

He is often reminded of the moment when his football coach in middle school decided to call him and his twin brother "Gonzales 1" and "Gonzales 2," because the coach either had an issue with their birth names or didn't care enough to learn. Being one of few persons of color in his high school, there was little opportunity for Alaa to share or even understand the depth and meaning of his experiences. How could he have known that the feelings he felt in that moment were valid? Were he and his brother the only student athletes singled out in this way? Could he predict that this would be the beginning of a string of similar future interactions with colleagues, patients, and caregivers?

What Alaa could not have begun to imagine was years prior to all of his confusing experiences, another individual on the other side of the world was living the same reality. His name was Rolihlahla. Zulu (2017) tells the story of Rolihlahla's first day of school in Africa and how his teacher was unable to pronounce his or any of the other students' African names. With a lack of authority, thought, or empathy, his teacher changed his name. Zulu informs that this act of naming can negatively affect the psyche in African populations and can be seen as an act of violence on the African mind. The name-changing process was carried out effortlessly and has continued for years. If the name Rolihlahla had been presented to the world along with his many contributions, would that have aided in more acceptance? What is important is that *he* knew his name. He knew it meant to "pull the branch of a tree" or "troublemaker."

Although born and raised in Oregon, Ohio (with a large Lebanese population located nearby in Toledo), Alaa's family roots began elsewhere. Alaa's mother was of Lebanese descent; however, she was born in São Paulo, Brazil. She and her family moved back to Lebanon, where she met Alaa's father. They left Lebanon together to return to Brazil, then to Toledo, starting their family in the United States. Alaa jokingly shares that he had a "typical meat and potatoes, apple-pie" American Midwest upbringing, in regard to his early beginnings. He is one of four brothers. Interestingly enough, Alaa still never felt as if he ever fitted in there. The "American upbringing" may have been naturally absorbed due to the environment he was in; however, his identity was being shaped long before he was born. Like many others striving toward the American dream, his identity was carried through the struggles of his parents. "You had pressure to succeed because you know what your parents told you they went through, so the sacrifices they made meant something." Alaa was a couple of weeks into his freshman year of college when the events on September 11, 2001 happened.

> "It changed everything for me. I went from walking through the world as a white boy to being a target. If you think the comments about my name were bad before, how do you think it went after 9/11? I am so glad my twin brother and I had each other. The anti-Arab and anti-Muslim rhetoric and discrimination was ridiculous. To be frank, it still is. But this opened up the floodgates in regard to my activism. I started putting together those awkward experiences I had growing up with the reality of the present. It's heavy stuff. The ongoing illegal occupation of Palestine and the illegal invasion of Iraq followed shortly after 9/11. Arabs and Muslims were the targets everywhere. I was afraid, but I was angrier, and speaking up became a method of survival. Before I even entered the OT world, I was organizing anti-war protests on campus and doing my best to speak truth to power."

Like their Jewish and Christian brothers and sisters, many individuals identify with Islam but do not practice the religion to its fullest. Cultural norms founded on the religion are passed down from generation to generation and, like the aforementioned monotheistic religions, Muslims come in all colors and from all ethnic backgrounds. "I feel I am ethnically Muslim. I don't necessarily believe in God, but I find myself gravitating toward Muslim customs and traditions. That's what I grew up with. I still don't eat pork, for example." Furthermore, with his name being confused with Allah, Alaa is part of Muslim rhetoric and culture, even when he might not want to be. This was a large part of his activism, defending Islam and Muslims.

Occupational therapy was not his original career path, but he couldn't help but be called to the profession after witnessing a therapist in action. "What the hell are you doing with the patient? Are you getting paid for this? Is this real?" The OT Alaa was shadowing, explained that he was working on problem-solving issues because of a frontal lobe injury acquired by the patient. Alaa never thought that the cognitive processes of playing checkers are also needed to complete more complex tasks such as making toast or executing a bathroom routine. It was at that moment Alaa admits, "I moved away from the sports aspect of things to the human aspect. Becoming an OT was the greatest thing I ever decided to do." Alaa left Ohio to pursue OT school in Philadelphia. "Occupation is liberation. We cannot engage in meaningful activity in a full way without liberation. So, what is meaningful to me and what is meaningful to you may not be the same, but we should definitely have the same chance at [participating in] it." Even as an OT student, Alaa noticed areas that were lacking in patient care. He reflected on the way OT practitioners would work with patients. "The way we talk about ADLs, the way we talk about meaningful activities is white centered. Things were said differently to people if the patient was white than if they were Black—lack of eye contact, bedside manner, even reports of pain."

Alaa is grateful that he was able to see this prior to completing his program so that he could have open conversations about it with his professors. What Alaa witnessed was nothing new but, in fact, possibly learned through the system of higher education. Olson and Burks (2022) continue to expose our current practices at the academic level regarding students and race. They remind us that systemic racism can be present in the university system because it was "founded by white men with white middle-to-upper class norms" (p.9). Furthermore, this system is embedded in the way staff present information and train students prior to them entering the workforce.

In this case, Olson and Burks point out the approach in which staff teach their content may be through their personal sociocultural lens, disregarding the range of cultures of students on the course.

Although the goal of occupational therapy is to assist patients in engaging and participating in meaningful activities, Alaa recognizes that "our profession has an individualism that is not okay, which is different from individuality, and is counterproductive." Olson and Burks (2022) urge that in order to increase diversity in our profession, we need to address how we are educating future occupational therapists. Occupational therapists work with many different people and professionals in order to obtain the best outcomes for their patients. This includes caregivers, family members, insurance companies, physicians, clinical psychologists, nurses, assistants, physical therapists, speech and language pathologists, the list goes on. In certain settings, an occupational therapist may work with some entities more than others. Alaa has had the opportunity to work in a plethora of OT settings, and is currently working in a hospital setting, where he collaborates with a large number of these professionals. Some of these interactions can create a great moment of triumph, but some moments are unsafe and dangerous.

In one example, Alaa had a technician with him to assist, to ensure safety of the patient and himself. He began to go over the case with the technician as well as what his plan would be to start the evaluation and intervention process. Alaa began by saying, "The patient has a gunshot wound with C-7 spinal cord injury, with no active movement from the waist down; however, she is responding relatively well." He went on to outline the plan of action, explaining, "We are going to try and do a circle sit with her, so I need your help to stay behind her. You can do a lot from a circle sit position, without having to reach very far." As Alaa continued to delve into the importance of the positioning of this patient and how they would benefit by gaining independence with bathing and dressing, the technician asked Alaa, "Is she Black?" Alaa was angry as he attempted to understand the reasoning behind the question. "This person just got shot in the neck and that was his first question?"

Alaa looked at the technician and bluntly stated, "You know what, man? I do not need you today, I'll go on my own." Alaa felt this was the right thing to do at the time, because the technician was heading into the session with a bias. "So, I went into the session and I did all that I wanted to do with her despite not having the second pair of hands, and I put myself at risk for injury. But I felt that taking the technician with me was less safe for the patient." Aside from having a successful session and the patient eventually being able to get into an acute rehab program to continue her recovery, there are still many areas in this scenario that could have been better. As professionals, we should be able to reflect on our own biases and find ways to set them aside in order to show up and be fully present for our team members as well as the patients we are serving. Isn't that why we entered the medical field to begin with, to serve others?

There was one particular case that brought joy and connection on different levels for Alaa. He had the privilege of being a part of a man's journey to recovery, which started out as a small accident and ended up being a very serious battle. We will call this patient Mohamed. Alaa remembers that Mohamed was visiting from Lebanon and he took a fall while visiting his family. He then had a stroke and had to go to the hospital and was later put on a ventilator. This patient improved and was medically stable, but not alert or oriented. Alaa explains, "I got a consult, but he was not responsive. They said, 'Hey, he speaks Arabic. Can you try?' He still was not responsive to Arabic or English. Nothing. A week and a half later I saw the patient's wife. She said he was doing better, so I went to say hi and his eyes were open. I said good morning in Arabic. The patient responded in Arabic!" Alaa was excited and took the steps to get Mohamed consulted for therapy again. It was a back-and-forth process, but the patient was able to follow commands and began physical therapy as well.

Alaa, along with a physical therapist, worked to provide the safest and most effective care possible and Mohamed started to respond to treatment. Over the next three weeks, Alaa had never used so much Arabic in his career. For two-hour sessions, five times a week, the cost for a non-insured patient from a foreign country was very high. Alaa remembers, "We had to work with social work and get a hold of the Embassy and everything. [His] wife ended up passing out from exhaustion; it was a mess. His visa expired and he wanted to go home but he couldn't." However, as a skilled occupational therapist, Alaa noted that he was doing well, but not well enough to fly. "I mean you think of occupation and activity analysis. We went as far as to teach him to transfer in and out of an airplane chair. We tried to make an airplane bathroom so he could turn and sit on a toilet in the tight little area on the plane." All of the time spent, the multiple consults, the collaboration with a myriad of health professionals and governmental entities, was all for one gratifying moment: "[His] wife ended up texting me from Lebanon on WhatsApp, a picture of him and his grandkids kickin' it. Full recovery."

Occupational therapists from all walks of life have had challenging and also very fulfilling experiences with their patient populations. Alaa's account of his unique moments are just samples of many. Could another occupational therapist connect with Mohamed like Alaa did? Would they have gone the extra mile to speak in Arabic if they could, or attempt countless times to get the patient into a therapy program? Or better yet, contact the Embassy? No one knows. What is for certain, is that Alaa was called "Gonzales 1" in middle school, he was looked at differently when 9/11 occurred, and his reality changed as he witnessed others in the medical profession marginalizing patients. Alaa concludes:

"As much as you want to be inclusive to your clientele, sometimes you overlook your therapeutic use of self and how important that can be. Not just with language but with empathy and comradery and solidarity and all the things that go into really being available for your patient. Not just using your cultural self but using your human self."

There is more to each of us than what is represented on our diploma, in our physical appearance, or in the letters on our name tag. We begin our lives as an extension of our ancestors and we develop into adulthood as a reflection of our environment, with more self-control for our response to this rather than for our process.

Our names signify a small piece of the inner complexities that make us who we are. Just as we teach young children to be themselves, this also includes their name, whatever name that could be. In this case, Alaa is his name and maybe one day, that will be enough. Just as Alaa has stayed true to his identity regardless of the perceptions of his name, so did Rolihlahla. Rolihlahla definitely stirred up necessary trouble in our world. Although his family, his tribe, and his ancestors gave him the name Rolihlahla for a reason, we have never known him as that. Nor have we seen his responses or actions when being called by his true name. Alaa perseveres daily to be called by his name. He exclaims, "I don't ask anyone to change who they are or what they are called." Maybe one day we will not have to change our true names in order to provide comfort for the person we are interacting with. Maybe one day, the textbooks will talk about Aladdin and his contributions to occupational therapy. Maybe one day, the history books will praise Rolihlahla and the impact he made on the world. For now, we will praise Rolihlahla and add his true name to the name we know: Rolihlahla (Nelson) Mandela. We have to start somewhere, right?

REFLECTION QUESTIONS

1. Have you ever experienced a time when you and your identity were dismissed or changed? How did it make you feel?
2. If you have not experienced this first-hand, have you witnessed a time where this has happened to someone else? How did you respond? And if you didn't, how could you in the future?
3. What's in a name? Does it matter to you if people call you what they want without your permission?
4. What kinds of changes can you impact globally when you start locally (within yourself)? What does that mean for those you will serve as an occupational therapist?

References

Olson, L.M. & Burks, K.A. (2022). Creating a racial and ethnic inclusive environment in occupational therapy education. *SIS Quarterly Practice Connections*, 7(1), 8–11.

Zulu, I.M. (2017). Synergizing culture: African American cultural recovery through African name. *Africology: The Journal of Pan African Studies*, 10(5), 128–154.